A Splash of Ink

A Splash of Ink
A personal collection of poems and micro-poems.

by
DAVID W BRYDON

Poetry: A Splash of Ink

Copyright © 2012 David W Brydon

Drawings Copyright © 2012 David W Brydon

All rights reserved.

No part of this book may be reproduced or transmitted in any form or by any means without written permission of the author

ISBN-13: 978-0-9880723-1-2 (Library and Archives Canada

ISBN-13: 978-09880723-0-5 (Library and Archives Canada) Electronic Version

ISBN-10: 0988072300

Book cover by Ryan McCarty: http://didj.deviantart.com
Drawings by Carmen and William Brydon

For my wife

Acknowledgments

I wish to personally thank the following people for their contributions, inspiration and for the infallible support they've provided me; without their belief in me, this book would never have been possible.

First and foremost, I want to thank my wife for all the support that she gave and continues to give me, not just during the writing of this book, but for all our wonderful years together. She is my life! This book is dedicated to her.

To my children, for all their love, patience, guidance and critical critiques of my poems and micro-poems; thank you!

Sonia Rumzi (http://soniarumzi.com) has supported my poems and encouraged me to write this book. She truly is a remarkable person.

Nicky Dijksman; Nicky's friendship has helped me move past what were once thought of as insurmountable challenges in life. Her personal support over the last several years has been instrumental and indeed the roots behind the rekindling of my poetry. In addition, this young women is a remarkable talent (www.youtube.com/dietcokewithcherry) in her own right and I strongly encourage everyone to support her endeavours!

Introduction

I actually wrote a cute little intro where I had 5-sentences; the first letter of each word was bold and spelt P.O.E.M.S. Okay, moving on.... ☺

So here's the reality - I'm under no pretence that I'm a poet of worth; quite the contrary. The majority of my work is pure crap - plain and simple. Having said that, the emotions and depth I try to express is indeed real, but sadly, I feel is unconveyed in words.

Perhaps, you'll note a progression as you quickly flip through the pages, but with poetry, it truly is each to their own likes and dislikes.

In summation, some of these poems are almost laughably bad, while others show mediocre potential at best.

Additionally, you may feel this intro, to be self-degrading. I see it as being my harshest critic.

However, if one can read between the lines and grasp the depth of meaning, then you may indeed find a few of my poems profound.

POEMS

The following entanglement of words, whether in a complete poem, or in the form of short micro-poems, are all mine and I take full responsibility for this mess. All my poems are original and usually written within minutes of inspiration; I rarely, if ever revise, so any misspellings or weird phrasing are clearly mine.

In regards to "micro-poems", you'll note they're scattered throughout the book and usually encapsulated within the markers "* * * * * *" indicated.

These small sparks of inspiration are simply that - and have nothing to do with any poem, unless specifically indicated. They are not joined to each other and separate in thought.

So let me welcome you inside my scattered head – be careful where you tread, as I've splashed ink.... everywhere.

My Saturated Stems

Although my roots are deep,
my mourning leans towards death;
drown these sorrows on the eve of a
silver lake, so I may sleep amongst my
earthen friends - long since gone,
to rest.

I reach with withered sticks,
tangled limbs towards grey
skies, crying - bare trunk,
once a soul, now left -
alone.

Swirling underneath,
such currents rage
this calm appearance,
surface, but a stage.

Twisted roots
Gnarled,
at the base
I can no longer
see ahead,
nor wish
to face.

My saturated stems.

* * * * * *

*What is flesh, if not the pains of love - that, which we crave - a
single touch
that starves our hunger*

I touch her – in whispered ways – until a hushhhhh is heard

She feels every word - and I feel…….. each breath…

In the wind, she blew a kiss – and it landed on…. his heart

*I need you – like you needed the apple – and delicious…… were
our sins*

*Our thoughts entwine – like lovers…. wrapped between pristine
sheets – this must be…
the purity… between our souls*

* * * * * *

Loves Due

He woke beneath a beating sun
to an afterglow of loves depart
as she washed away his worries
on tides, now held at bay.

Then she kissed him in the light of moon
and in the darkness of his day.

Suppressing kindled fires
stacked upon clay pots
smoldered, were the arms that wrapped
now charcoaled - his phosphorous thoughts.

Yet steam billowed from the sails
white foam, splayed across depth of draft
as he coursed through…. rough seas
she watched his heart bail.

What more could she give
but hold her love, to his course true
he'll navigate this jealous remorse
to understand, loves due.

* * * * * *

Shy.... is my morning sun - peeking through the clouds.... she leans ~ to kiss my tender earth

I send you my heart.... to set you free - while asking you...... to hold the beat...... which will lead you – to me

Shall I hold you tonight – only till the last star.... fades into the mornings light – then just a little longer – until the moon begins to sing again.... to the night

* * * * * *

When The Wolves Howl

When the wolves howl, at the moon
I listen
I am awake

It's when they howl in my mind
that I wish I were asleep

My mind is my refuge
I am a romantic
I am dramatic
I am an insomniac
I simply am

Who I am

---
*See Authors Note 1

Shadows

From the shadows peers my past,
round the corner up at last.

Twinges, flashes, sparks, and ashes,
deep within the shadow passes.

Fire burning from within - glasses tipped,
full of gin while old men sitting often grin,
knowing well, the turmoil in.

Shadows hidden for the day,
glowing embers close at bay.

Twinges, flashes, sparks, and ashes,
darkness full, then the clashes.

Hollow nights, begin to swallow,
surrounding madness, cold and hollow.

Twinges, flashes, sparks, and ashes,
Morning rises…..
and the shadow passes.

---

*See Authors Note 2

* * * * * *

She hid behind her words, like lies behind the sun – shadows in the darkness…. She was always… on the run

When you die, I'll go sit - by the river – until the waters still – & my shadows pass – then I'll rest with you – below the rivers bed

Dimly I sit…… beneath the dark - fathoms of the deep - a phantom to myself…… this mask - shadows, which I keep

Life threads its way~~~~~ to my broken heart – to a tear along my soul – the very fibre…. of who I am - and lost so long ago

* * * * * *

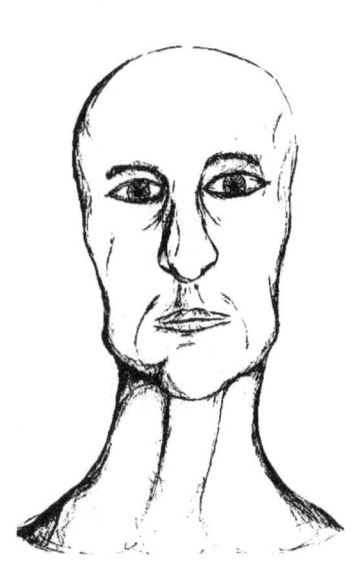

Taste The Fear

The earth raised
beneath me
logic was unclear
the only thing
for certain was,
that I could taste the fear.

A mile away,
I just can't say
I turned to see my home
remarkable, still standing
a vision, made from stone.

No pain, nothing…
but unsupportable loss.

Flung through the air
slowing down the motion
with plenty of time
to stare.

A man can be reached
when clearly in the breach
a quick reflection of the
soul
then becomes
a primary goal

especially, when sounds
begin to screech.

Then it slipped away
all the air was gone
leaving me at bay.

Choking, spitting spewing
left sitting in a hole
nothing left around,
but little chunks of coal.

Inflating breast
to expand command
no point in sitting there
with nothing left,
worth a stare
didn't really give a damn
just being honest with you
there.

The only thing for certain
was, I couldn't bloody
well hear -
but I sure as hell
could taste the fear.

* * * * * *

*If I looked through a window... what would I see – not the pains of you –
but a reflection .... of me*

I know your silence, and you speak it - with conviction

In his darkest nights... he raises arms... to wave away these memories – but in the light of day.... he see's - that they're ingrained..... within his hands

* * * * * *

Do I Still Exist

Hanging from a rope
watching people...pass by
who are they -
doesn't matter
I only want....
to watch the fading sun.

Can you kiss me now
hold me in your arms
I only want a moment
to rest....on a bed of hope.

I waited
but you were late
when you ran to me
I had a ticket
on a different plain
to destiny.

Now free from ambiguity
the question is - -
do I still exist.

---

*See Authors Note 3

* * * * * *

Broken glass...... reflecting past - his shattered red stained eyes - he slips by the human race - no humanity...... on their quickened pace

He closes his eyes, to fields of grey, while bitten by the earth - he lays - as tears tumble down.... and they too.... roll away

* * * * * *

Days Ago

A portrait of life you see
turmoil ridden, lost at sea
German wine and French Béarnaise
Jumping Frogs and twisted days

I tumbled down a stair or two
while looking back at you

Intoxicated and besot
I wobbled round and drunk allot
those twisted tortured days of haze

A portrait of a life you see
not always what you want it to be
German wine and French Béarnaise
Jumping Frogs and twisted days

Many days ago.

———————
*See Authors Note 4

Metal Closet

In a locked metal closet,
compartmentalised away.

My mind was kept,
yet did not stay.

Grey and wet, and dark,
you see, it was always
kept confined.

Tucked away in recesses,
down deep and hollow
rows;
a shelve so far away.

Nothing could have
reached it, nor dare to go
that far.

Yet the pressure built
from all those years, and
the ebb began to flow.

The pace began to
quicken,

the blood began to pound.

Raging through the veins
so fast, up and through,
and then the crash.

Outward poured the
anger held, spilling forth
this much was clear.

A blackened tar, of fear.

An echo of the past was
here,
I never wished to see.

The clunk of metal locked,
is all I want to hear.

Throw the bloody key
away,
and stem the raging fear.

———

*See Authors Note 5

* * * * * *

You call yourself a present… wrapped up in your eyes –
but the value in a gift – is much deeper…. then the bow

My sleeves are bare, my heart is torn - a severed thread – – now
forlorn

* * * * * *

Forever Longed

The first giggled kiss
where eyes close…
and our hearts pound.

Where excited hands
and fingertips
caress the sweetness -
of her velvet lips.

Hold my neck
hands through hair
a vision of beauty
the reality…..
we shared.

That one sweet kiss
in loving arms -
held in memory
and
forever longed.

Silver Moon

Like a silver moon
watching time disappear
the midnight flame of life

Dancing in my mind
of thought
distorted by the light

She slipped behind my
armoured shell
attacked my heart and
mind

Plucking strings
like a banjo man
on the front porch keeping
time

She struck a chord with
words
crashing through my skull
battling emotions
waves against the hull

Like a silver moon
watching time disappear
the midnight flame of life

Head pressed against the
door
braced against her will
She whispered through
the crack
I'll be waiting for you still

Like a silver moon
watching time disappear
the midnight flame of life

She's had her days
and will not get in
until the morning rises
and the sins are washed
away

Like a silver moon
watching time disappear
she'll simply fade away.

* * * * * *

*You are my summer – my warm blue sky – you are the river~~~~~
of my soul – you are my… golden meadow – in life*

* * * * * *

All These Dots

The hardest thing to do
is to simplify what's true
with all these dots, which
connect me to you.

An outline of a vision
on the eve, of this division
ink spots - galaxies,
a space away, and
a picture looms.

I turned a leaf,
a side unseen
then began to draw
these lines between.

All these dots,

with curves…
a puzzle in the end.

This sketch of what
could have been,
yet never seen
a cluster
of the stars between.

The hardest thing to do
is to simplify what's true.

Regardless,
each dot connects me
to you.

* * * * * *

*Her fingers interlace, with rude thoughts, which trace -
the outline------— of his imagination*

*I am a dreamer – I watch the stars…. and croon…. to the moon –
I am the tree…. by the river*

*If sleep were a woman……. I would surrender myself - to her sweet
charms*

*The river flows deep – between the loins of the earth – as does my
love…. for her*

* * * * * *

Unlike The Seed

In the mix
of the battle fought
the carnage.......
burroughs deep.

Unlike the seed
it drinks the soul
and withers –
the leaves of mind.

Until the tree of man
is fell.

* * * * * *

He falls into a hole - too deep to know - and overhead the sun begins to fade.... does his life, have nothing left to say

Dark is the surrounding light, which cuddles his despair – but crisp is the midnight air..... to cleanse the breath of life

Her sweet tendrils of breath -------- — traced through the air ------- until they found...)))))))... his kiss

I like to watch the wind.... and listen to the leaves – I like to feel her hands... on me – a sensation... which takes my breath~~~~ away

* * * * * *

Just Listen

Please - please listen,
just for this…one
moment…
listen…..
I ask nothing more…
but listen

Shhh, please…shh….
listen - listen…LISten
Dammit!
ahhhh - Just Listen -
…listen…please
please…

Listen to my heart
that's all I ask - listen to
my heart
listen to it beat, feel it beat
it beats for you, always
you… just you

Give me your and…
please
it's okay, look…
place it here - on my chest

just listen….shhh, listen
can you feel it - it's you
it beats for you

Tell me - what do you
hear….ahhhhh…..
yes…it's my heart - my
heart
….my heart - it's breaking
-
it's breaking….

It's breaking….for you

Just listen - just listen

Can you hear it now

Its breaking apart…for
you

please….

just listen

Eyes Open

My eyes opened
wide and wild
I stilled my heart
held my breath
wanting to expel
night thoughts

Fingers cling to sheets
stabilizing my world

Close the shutters
to my soul
Don't breathe
still.... Be still...
flow backwards
like the ebb of the tide
washing away the night

cleansing the beach
clearing the debris
of dreams

Reclaim the moment
strip the darkness, and
regain your light of day

Eyes open
safe
heart stilled - calm
sigh of breath
aching bones
expelling death

Alive

* * * * * *

Charcoal to wall - pencil to paper - paint to canvas.... I drew her

~~~~

so she'll be close ...... to me

*How drunk are you...... to swill these men – that you've drank
in...... all their sorry hearts –
and shattered...... all their dreams*

* * * * * *

Words

Once a word has left, the chamber
there's nothing, which can be done.

Running along the edge,
of a blade
sharp as a pointed tongue
slipping -
now looking down the barrel,
of a smoking gun.

Awkward is the moment
the sulphur in the air
Black powder, lead against
thin paper [hanging] in the air,
bleeding words
left dripping smudges
under eyes..., of despair.

No eraser can retract
words sent flying
heard so clearly, so exact.

If one could only rewind
smoke to lead, lead to barrel
words locked and chambered, in the narrow
..., a passage, tightly tucked away.

Then nothing else
would need to be said...
this day

Sand

I lay there, feet in sand
hands buried in thought
turning grains of time.

Eroded bits, slipping
off my mind, crumbling
to the dance and pounding
of the age-old waves,
as the sea rushes in.

Ticking, one single grain
slipping through, my fingers
quartz crystals,
the hourglass of time.

Drenched in brine
white foam, flushing mind
pockets underneath,
collapsing, by one piece…
a grain at a time
slithering away, with the tide,
backwash of the sea, and mine.

I lay there, feet in sand
hands buried in thought
turning grains of time.

Life, washing thoughts back to sea
giving time back - by
polishing my soul and me.

* * * * * *

My candle is dim... and my passion near death - - - where is.... my love....
and loves last breath....

I look at you..... like a wild flower.... looks up....... at the sun

She is my petalled rose.... my love - and I, her stem – I hold her to the light –
so everyone.... can see her bloom

When I touch your hand - you touch my heart

She is – the road I wish to travel – and the journey..... I never wish to end

Sometimes I'm lost – stuck-out – on a limb without an end – but if I can find my way to you – then I'll be home.... again

I love her – like the rain~~~~~ loves the water

* * * * * *

Swallows Even Me

Twilight, soft and diffused
daily thoughts become confused

The blackness of the night you see
swallows even me

Breathtaking from the heart
building caves, deep and stark

Vagueness begins to loom
thoughts of day turn to gloom

The blackness of the night you see

Swallows even me...

* * * * * *

*When I was one and twenty, there was no light of day - for
everything I seen......
was in the darkness - of a midnight...... cabaret*

*Can you imagine what it's like - to feel your dreams – cuddled...
in the middle of your stormy nights...*

*With a wet brush, dipped in tears, he paints; deep into a
corner...unsure and unaware......
of where... the shadows stand*

* * * * * *

Still Just Me

My best days are when your name
is tasted on my lips. But when I call
to you, and sense the feeling of your dread,
what am I to say –
when my lungs collapse
and all the air.... has left.

But now I'm full of doubt
and everything I felt
is draining..... fast away -
but if I could reach across the street
you'd see.... that it's still -
just me.

* * * * * *

She built a wall of silence, a siege is underway; I cannot fathom such despair -
perhaps a ladder...... so she can hear me.... in the clear

Your lips caress the air I breathe – and my hope one-day - - -
is that they'll...... caress me

Crisp, the morning air ~ a refreshing, drink of life ~ breathing out despair

How can I dry your tears – on the sorrow of my heart – how can you not drown.... within my own

No keys on my chain – will open your door – for your heart is like a fridge - - so cold inside

* * * * * *

Breathless

I ran the length
a trench
within my mind

Shattered thoughts
strewn about
never would I find

Motionless, as still
as fear
breathless
death was near

Crawling now
along the pit
water deep to lips
gasping, listening
motionless
breathless,
fearing that I would slip

Without a breeze
no thoughts to cleanse
a mind, so deep in mud

Lay within the trench
I dug,
now breathless
gasping for a nudge.

To Me

On the edge, I stood
just shy of all the rocks
filtered mind of gravity
pulling down my socks
stripping back…,
- exposing me.

Toe to water
silt to sand
I wondered,
where and when
it all began.

Closing eyes
and turning head
I woke before the noon
off to walk and left to ponder
underneath the blackest moon.

Then I thought within my mind
what a busy place to be
so I stopped!
Just so I could see.

In the crowd, I stood alone
surrounded by myself
then she waved and
danced for me
this pirouette of hope and self
buried beneath my
crashing sea
of humanity and me.

A sparkle and a maiden
whom I could always see
And really,
that's all that mattered

To me.

* * * * * *

*In the darkness of his mind, he reached out - when a smile appeared
- it was the sweet touch…… of her caring hand*

*She had a sharpness to her tongue - peeling back the quiet
sheath….. of lips - she cut him---- with her words*

* * * * * *

Languish

Dizzy - walking off the line
like a heavy fog
I no longer see the signs.

Through the gate
like an off kiltered weight
balanced undefined
swinging...on hinges
unfocused in my mind.

A creak, a groan
an occasional moan
left with cornered thoughts
while sitting all alone.

Languishing with visions
in this palatial mind
compartmentalized
broken and divided
filled with echoes never heard
nor words defined.

In this mind, I languish
and pine away...
yearning for a life I bought
with my underpinning thoughts
besotted and with fears
as I languish in my ways
for those much more
simpler days.

Close my eyes

Draw the bow across my heart
with dancing fingers
sliding strings alive, my ears
lovingly abide.

I sit and close my eyes
listening to the tunes
just off to my side
floating through the air,
removing my despair.

A gentle voice, a soothing choice
of notes…, which filter across my way
worries, sliding off, dissipating
like dew on a summer morning day.

To quietly sit, not to fidget or fit
no mental strategies or wit
but a single moment for me
to wash away all my worries and
chaos of the day
just to sit and listen for a bit…

So draw the bow across and sing
use your dancing fingers
to gentle pry apart
those withered strings upon my heart
to make my ears come alive and lovingly abide
as you wash away my worries
while I sit and close my eyes.

* * * * * *

*Can I kneel beside you - a quiet reverence paid; my head, upon
your delicate heart......
is laid - till death*

*He fears not death, but suffers life; the fool that he is —
which she endures*

*Hold me like death —
grip me like the earth —
embed me in you….. as if we were one —
then…… then we shall live*

*Before you die, I'll hold you — I'll wrap you in my arms…. and kiss
you — until the last note…. of the piano……. fades away*

*I slice these wrist — so I can pour my blood~~~~~ upon the
starkness of your page — for you are the very ink…… within me*

* * * * * *

*Humanity — now only a whispered word
spoken in the darkest part of night
terrified — are the politicians
who have fallen asleep
huddled in their leather chairs
afraid to been seen
in the backrooms
of light*

* * * * * *

Tattoo's

In the evening sun,
the drum beats,
calling them home,
soldiers feet, tapping
rhythmic thumping
like a heartbeat.

The motor whirls
needles vibrate
the beat of the drum,
gliding, piercing,
pigmented into the skin

Like a machine gun
raking across our flesh,
pounding ink into the
soul.

The priest blesses the
soldier
the tattoo blesses the skin
magical protection
warding off demons of the
night of the mind, within.

She remembers.

In the evening sun,
the drum beats,
rhythmic thumping

inking her skin

Circles of life
enveloping and protecting
her soul

Stars, for the heavenly
bodies
to navigate safely through
the celestial stars of our
universe

Numbers - numbers...
like the beat of the heart,
in time with the drum
to count the souls

Like the soldiers
tapping their feet
called home

to the tattoos
evening beat -

She remembers.

———

*See Authors Note 6

I Remember Them

Hell rising from the sea, with
churning swells of bellies and steel beasts
spewing raging storms of heat
piercing cries of overlord beseeched.

They ran the beaches with pounding feet
friends left, not but three feet,
amongst the frothy deep, of the channel sea.

Left to prepare the landings of despair,
as the heavens weep; all this bleeding life on foreign streets,
so very far from home…
as mothers sent their boys, no choices left, they faltered,
falling to their knees, thinking - stop this bloody madness…
please.

Up the Scheldt, to flooded lands, boots wet, muck of mind,
with drowning sorrow not knowing what they would find.
These men of yesteryears, fought struggles, for the hearts…,
of those people they never knew, with their tears, muddy on
their cheeks, and like them on their minds… and souls.

Trudging on, not so very long ago, they made a difference,
which we now know; and I remember them!

I remember them.

Concentration

Railed and jammed, trenched in bile, choking my concentration; buried deep in stench, now spiraling up, lost is life's hope.

Shattered were there numbered days, striped with prejudices - war and torn.

Crimson edge, along this darkness bleeds; decay, black with dampened eyes, stripped bark and skin that sheds.

Wires barbed with teeth, chomping at the bit; greyed louses, boots, which stomp and kick, ordered by their blacken threads.

Then washed away to
sodden grounds,
unearthed beneath
the sky - where
dreams have laid,
withered, crushed by
fools, left limp and
dying, amongst the
living dead.

On top of lime and
soiled earth,
we now tromp a daily tread –
to death.

An Old Stone Well

An old stone well
Stained water, deathly brown
reflecting back
shimmering ~~~, from my past
...eerie still, as I peer down.

A single tear
Salt from eye to mouth
this briny taste, fallen over time
waiting, for a ripple to appear.

Leaning over, a sickly draft,
gagging on a cry,
wafting up, this stench of past
of an escaping, echo sigh.

Slipping past my lips
down the mossy walls,
which I...
built high, over the weight of time
now dripping,
these hollow stone piles,
deep within my mind.

Looking, into this old stone well
with creaking, rusty pump
spewing dust...,
into an empty bucket...
of thoughts,
left chipping at the crust.

One step back,
And up I look,
A refreshing breath, I took!
This well, is old - dank and cold,
It's the sun I need in life.

Breathing deep,
I walk away,
Never looking back,
At that old stone well
Where I once choked, and sat.

We'll Be Fine

In the middle of time,
everything stops
Two hands dancing,
between the time
and the clock
Third wheel spinning still.
A slice, half part me, the
other you.
Can this be true?

Midnight divides us,
Worlds collide at the
strike of dawn
Separated by Greenwich
Mean and you
Stuck in the London
Tower of mine.
Watching time, our heads
on a pole, life's end of
day, crossing from this
side to the west.

If I could hold you, thighs
to thighs
Hinged between the time,
and eyes
Embers of your light of
day

My darkness stripped
away
Like numbers on the face,
of time
Slowly passing, as each
moment ticks
this is my sublime, these
mental tricks
of time and mine.

The motions of clock, and
the mind spinning round
and locked
With jumping hands from
me to you, and kisses on
the face, places moist with
grace
In-between the time of
you and me
We'll be fine, in the
middle of this moving sea.

When everything stops,
Two hands dancing,
between the time
and the clock,
we'll be fine, just you and
me, and time.

Lonely Thoughts

Sheltered,
I stand and watch
with overhanging thoughts
…reaching out
extending…
well beyond my reach.

Loneliness appears
in single pains
each framed,
dripping… with my tears.

A salty brine
mixed…
Then washed away -
in time.

* * * * * *

His heart beats, to a lonely chest which aches - the only thumps,
are moist little drips….. of his internal sighs

Tears in a jar – a glass bubble of life –
these shattered emotions and fragments of fears –
splinters dripping from his timbered years

I once wrote her a letter….. with a hammer in hand - to bear
witness, to where I stand; cold steel, which burns……… my lonely
heart

* * * * * *

Just Her And I, And Me

We used to sit,
underneath the tree.
Just her and I, and me

Summer nights,
seemed so sweet.
Innocent and bright,
as we sat underneath
the lights.

Upon the grass,
leaning against the poll,
my mind would whirl,
of thoughts of her and I.

Just me you see,
in my mind,
of her and I.

Oh, too laugh and play,
they were grand old days,
Just her and I, and me.

Under that lamp,
leaning against the pole,
dreams were made,
and told.

I held her hand,
sweaty and cold,
but the warmth, was
unmistakable, the
movement
young and bold.

Her eyes, oh...,
how they would twinkle,
starlight's in her soul.
She made me feel so good,
lighting up my dreams,
everything I did,
she said - I knew you
could.

Winter came and days
went by, only choice, was
to sit and stare, and watch
our dreams go by.

Days, and months and
years,
fly by.

I sit and wonder why.
I should have asked her
then,
rather than say goodbye.

Now I sit and think,
poor me,
it could have been,
Just her and I.

Swish Swish… swish

Walking merrily along
one day, I thought I heard
a noise

I stopped and glanced
about
but heard nothing,
as I poised

Hmmm I thought,
strangest thing is that

Pitter patter off I go,
down the lane again.

Swish Swish swish

What the hell is that, I
said!

Did you hear that?
Well yes I did, said my
dog
looking at me funny.

Squinting eyes, I look
about
peering at my shoes.

Nothing there I think,
and off I go,
swishing down the street.

Well, that's it I said,
surly a joke am I, as I spy
about.

I lift one foot, then the
other,
nothing I can see, but me
standing like a fool, in the
middle of this city sea,
with people all about.

Swish Swish swish again.

What's this all about.

On the bottom of my shoe
you see, was a two-way
piece of tape, sticking to
the ground, then sticking
it to me.

———

*See Authors Note 7

Just Another Gnome

What compels me
to find those things
what sunset do I seek
what avenues to walk
is destiny a corner
just around the block
do cobblestones meet pavement
or does the dirt road
always lead to rock
am I lost
will I ever be the same
should I wander past the stars
have I travelled too far
what compels me
to search for you
to find my nook of heaven
cradled in your breast
kiss the splay of pedals
until you lay at rest
do the fires burn
does such a life exist
will I find the flames
or burn in hell
while they laugh at me in jest
can I find my way back home
or toil in the garden -
as just another gnome.

* * * * * *

I don't want you to be lost - but I too...want to be found

I mourn her, like a ghost ship, lost at sea - tossed and turned, rusted -
this empty shell...... of me

* * * * * *

Keeping Me From Rest

If I arch to you
I feel the studs behind the wall
and you soak into my mind.

I watch as your eloquence
befalls you
when you enter from the gloom.

Then your shadow falls on me
like a long unrest -
torn from a sleepless night.

You bathe me, while I wait
scratching shutters across my chest
ravishing my body
slipping between the sheets...unseen.

Keeping me from rest.

* * * * * *

Take me by the hand….. and cradle me to you – listen…. and feel my beating heart – as it beats for you

Each day I rise - and hope to see the sun - it doesn't matter if it rains or not - it's the light within her eyes…. I want

* * * * * *

Picture by Paula Langezaal ©
http://myblog-ancientone.blogspot.com

* * * * * *

He only ask for comfort - a shoulder soft of thought - an understanding of a life - and the challenges.... he's overcome - and fought

His bones turned to Jelly - when his heart was crushed - as she sat..... and enjoyed the marrow

One word – one solitary word….. from her – is like a book of love – and she's the only thing in life…. I need to read

* * * * * *

Leap of Faith

A leap of faith
within confines
while tethered
to the ground.

I jump!

With effort, I float
pined….
in my virtual cage
surrounded
by my hope.

Dried and withered
trying… to break free
through concrete
and….
across my vision
I can see

The colour of life
and the greenery
with…
a leap of faith
life begins
just beyond the trees.

No Matter What I Say

Still wind on a summer's eve,
drenched moonlit sleeves, like
spotlights on the side of walk;
lighting paths, which focus on our talks.

A step, a stretch, astride, straddling
discussions, unwilling to abide.
Normalcy, pleased and clipped, then
dipped in cosmic gin, expanding thoughts
releasing synergy, as planets of ideas align.

She curtsies and I bow, unsure of how,
but realizing the end is near, one foot off
the curb, a lip a curl and a sneer. But one thing
for sure is clear - the wit of her cynicism
has dipped her brow and beaten, questions
risen, claiming fowl - despite my claims
it was not a chicken, but a hen.

And so it goes, the walk was over,
the sky and moon have closed.
No more thoughts to buy or bid, and
then she said - good riddance
this is clearly - The End.

Because, no matter what I say,
I just can't seem to win.

Twelve beers

Twelve beers on a Halifax night
Dripping from the pubs
Spitting off the pier
Tall ships in the harbour
Sails full, seagulls in flight
I missed her in my dreams
Passed out, on a cold bloody night.

White waves, saying goodbye
Tides out, as I open my eyes
Captain is yelling,
Where the hells my first mate.

Pissing in the wind
First shower of the day
Hands combed through the hair
Not an aspirin in site
Thank god for no mirrors
After that cold bloody night.

Up on the Citadel, all out of breath
Leaning on canons, smoke entering my chest
There she is, out pass the fort
by McNab, well out the port, off to deep sea.

Twelve beers on a Halifax night
Dripping from the pubs
Spitting off the pier.

But across the way
A warm bed and a lass
I missed her in my dreams
Those tall beams and a mast
On wavy blue nights, we would dance to a jig
Hanging high in the rig,
winds howling a tune
I'm hoping I'll see that old girl soon.

Twelve beers on a Halifax night
Dripping from the pubs
Spitting off the pier.

* * * * * *

Back of mind…… a big hollow pit - for tossing useless thoughts……
I should jump in…… to see what's left to find - within

A ball of twine, wrapped too tightly –
in sloshing mental brine……
unraveling knots, and an idea caught –
yet unable to define

He reacted – what else could he do - a mental loop - a rotation of a hoop -
he had no choice…… but to jump through…

Shards beneath my feet; broken is the class when walked upon -
like a fragile heart, which beats…

Can you hold me - like the dark….. holds the night – or love me –
like the morning…. loves the song – of the doves

How can I breathe…… when you treat me – like a stranger – you
tear away my lungs…. then you take away - my heart

Am I the zebra…..in the middle of the field – or is all you see…. is
the horses – which surround me

She watches – as the tired moon….. droops past the dawn – and
the clouds hide – deep within…. her shadowed eyes

* * * * * *

Twenty-one

I filled the space between
the words
with Inner thoughts,
seldom heard
I sang the songs to keep
away
Crimson mind of bloody
days

When I was twenty-one

Then she came from in the
shade
To fix the life that I had
made
Why don't you tell your
story to me
of things you never say
I'll listen to you
I want to hear
you know I do, I promise
you

Because I am twenty-one

You're one day up and
two away
it doesn't matter I'm here
to stay
At some point, you need
me close
You know you do, and so
do I

My earth trembles when I
hear
what you did so far away
those things you never say

Because of days when you
were twenty-one

So put your heart in my
hand to stay
Together we'll try to find
a way
Lets fill those spaces
which words can't say

If I were twenty-one

One Breath at a Time

This weight of life, bearing down
Soundless in such pressure found
upon his chest, barely a breath -
he takes - laying on this hill of life
a heap of a mess, he's built, and
piled it on his very own chest.

One hundred stories, he lay beneath
arms raised in why, tears streaked
flat of man, his life squeezed out
unbearable weight, this terrible clout.

It's clear, he has surely lost his way,
His realization, late of day.
Silence in the sounds, nothing left around
This seems to be the way; left thinking,
he has little left to say.
No breath, with life upon his chest
He gave up, not wishing to be found.
.....
She looks up to see him sitting there
An old man without a peep, no tales
Nor does he speak, nothing but tears
Stained upon his withered cheeks

Sitting by his side, looking deep into his eyes
She clasps his hand, and warmly says
One breath at a time, one blue sky a day
Let's sit a bit - and wash away that grey.

After a while, she turned to him and kissed his cheek;
releasing such a sigh, he looked at her
as if in wonderment and why.

You have no weight upon your chest
You simply need to breathe.
You built a pile, filled with life
Then sat a while, forgetting how to smile.
Sitting tall, his shoulders back he looked at her
and said - you gave me life, and breathe this day
and washed away the dirt of life, which held me to my strife,
when I had lost my way.
One breath at a time, one blue sky a day
Can we sit a bit - and enjoy this wonderful day.

* * * * * *

Who can imagine - a child, who grows old… and life fraught…
with life - a young mind, which withers of age - at the end of day

I know your secrets - but will you let me in.... to feel your pain

Beneath the years of age, a structure found - solid to the core; an
echo sounds....)))) reminding me…… of my past

You hide…. when you close your eyes – so what am I to do…..but
wait – watching out the window – as all my flaws~~~ float by

Why do you crave…. my weakness – and desire all my sins – while
I don't understand… your temptations – I do desire you… and
them

* * * * * *

Shattered

You stood glaring
through a glass plate window
watching from behind.

Then you shattered me
and walked on by
knowing you'd be fine.

A distorted life
of rippled panes
thinking...I would never
be the same
I should have seen
the signs.

I was but a platform
for you within a bed
never understanding
all the pains you caused
while standing on my head.

Everybody suffers
but why'd you take my
soul
it wasn't yours, but mine
now I have no choice
I'll have to find rewind.

You know you did
you shattered me

choked me with your
shards
but like you, I'll find a
way
to spit you out
discarding what you say
and unplug you, from my
mind.

Then I'll walk away.

* * * * * *

But every love comes with pain ~
each soul is different ~
not everyone's the same ~
but what victories......
have been lost

Nothing but the moon is bright, in the middle of my wanting
night; if I could only howl......
to keep things - at their bay

His heart was out of tune –
worn strings...... frayed –
the minstrel of his soul...... has lost the beat –
the silence may soon be...... complete

I like to watch the wind....and listen to the leaves – I like to feel her
hands...on me –
a sensation...which takes my breath away

Her kiss.... like the wind – always leaves me........ brrreathless

Slipping between my arms...... pinned against my chest –
a sensations...... unlike the rest...
with a sprinkling –
of you

The gravity of her...... weighs on me - but I cherish...... each
gram of flesh...... and will carry her - forever - and a day

* * * * * *

I Remember You

A spiraled bound book
with pages lined
I draft words, longed....
on these sheets of time.

From memories
dredged, deep within
stored in hidden corners
held together, by fingers
and bow wrapped twine.

To remember you
on rainy days
of the sunshine
in our youthful ways.

I remember you
when our love was young
of the giggles had
and the stories told.

So I pen to you
each day of life
my love....
as we grow old.

And I long for you
in this story -
I've now told.

* * * * * *

*My inner soul....pines for you - like leaves in the tree....
pine for the wind*

Can you not hold my heart but once – and I..... yours..... forever

* * * * * *

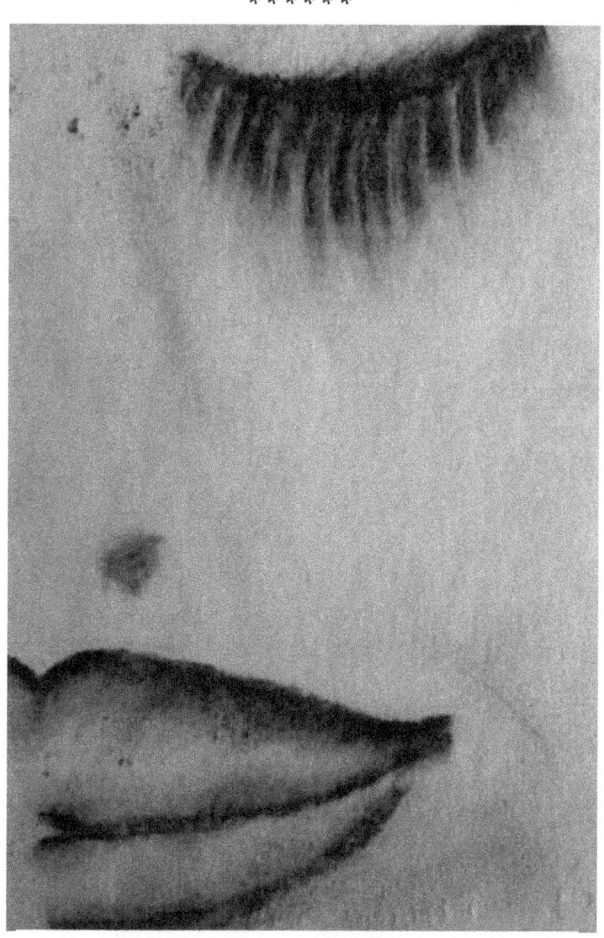

Picture by Paula Langezaal ©
http://myblog-ancientone.blogspot.com

In The Leaves

In the middle of the yard
I found a seat
just beneath the rustling
of my tired... feet.

Quietly I listened
as my thoughts....
began to slow
remembering the days
not that long ago.

Between my toes
I watched...
these dancing leaves
twirling acrobats
traipsing
in the morning's breeze.

Her and I
that's who we were
carefree,
like syrup song-birds
smooth and sweet.

I stood-up
and grasped the rake
twirling with a smile
I kissed the morning wind
and danced....
amongst the pile of
memories.

Such freedom, in the
clarity
and beauty - of the
moments seen
these gracious
opportunities
while sitting...
in the leaves.

* * * * * *

We met by chance, a fleeting glance, under a falling moon.
She blew a kiss, which nearly missed, but now we reminisce

Filtered moon above ~ cloudy are the skies… behold ~ beauty, in the grey

Remove his bark and steep his thoughts, which brew into a midnight dark;
stew until a mornings light, when only his supple grains - remain

* * * * * *

My Life

How far I've come
but that's not me
down this narrow hall
which peers.

I stoop
to get a better look
was it a race
did I win
where are my friends.

An effort to discern
clearly…

I've been left behind
forgotten
now bound - to mind.

My life
pressures I did bear
wilting
I sit alone
now wishing …
I were anywhere
-
but here.

Words we spoke

My heart was torn upon your soul
you wretched it from the depth
if the only promise you had kept
in the bed where we had slept.

The morning sun and gentle breeze
twilight moons, oceans and the seas
gentle caresses – weak at knees
thrashing heart and clinging pleas.

Lies beneath the autumn leaves
colours changing as you please
solitude and respite
drunk upon your very sight.

Meaning what I ask you now
as I flow upon the street
I only ask you ever keep
the words we spoke upon our meet.

* * * * * *

She hid behind her words, like lies behind the sun – shadows in the darkness....
She was always...... on the run

I whisper dreams into her ears......... but deaf...... is her replies - of reality

* * * * * *

In The Waiting Room

She stood by, while I watched
no words shared, no choice
no option, but to stand
and stare.

We looked upon
this naked scene
unsure of how it started
or began...

One foot forward
the other...well
it was way beyond
then I tried
to catch my breath
realising then
I had forgotten to dress
except the tie, the knot too tight.

But that's okay
as everything
turned out .... alright.

Anyway, here we are
in the middle of the mix
bit of a swoosh and a
swish
but no sleeves or tricks.

Just so you know

it all began in the womb
then the next thing I knew
I was there, many years
later
myself, standing ...
in the waiting room.

A Wall

What is a wall,
what is a brick
Substance thick
I cannot breathe -
my vision blurred
I yell and yell,
no longer am I heard.

Slathered,
in-between the layers
dividing those who stare
the living veins of mortis
a rigor without a care.

Stoned and stained,
Higher, higher, higher,
when will it stop!
left splattered with distain
superior… above the pain
–
It will not.

We assume,
that everyone knows -
what we know
a division at the top
built upon a foot
a leg[acy] of stone.

A wall, a wall a wall
no longer can I stretch
I cannot see beyond the
tall.

Then I climbed
to look and see
beyond the media
beyond the me
and there it was…
Normalcy!

Just over the edge
a wall, of humanity.

* * * * * *

I watched, as each grain…… ticked - - - by; whirling sands of time,
now slowed -
moments caught…… on the reels of mind

* * * * * *

Spilt Emotions

In the moment, all is fine
a cleared table
and a steady mind.

But in a flash
the drapes are closed
and hidden is the sun
-
there's nothing left
and nothing to see
so he begins, to run….

Near the edge
he reaches out
all in the hope… to find.

But then he trips
on his misguided mind
shattered, is the glass
spilt emotions
are now
dripping….
past
his edge.

* * * * * *

I stand behind a curtain ///// waiting….. for my mental play - to start

* * * * * *

Let The Roses Grow

You're not invisible to me
I see your hidden tears
trapped beneath and
tucked away, for all those
dripping years

But then I found your rain
barrel, right beside my
house
an over flowing mess
now running fast and
soaked
deep into my past.

Now standing on these
marshy thoughts
I dwell, wringing time,
now drenched, no longer
can I say or tell the
difference in the
curvatures of barrel
stave's from your
weighted spine.

In support, I kneel to you
wrapping rugged steel
hooped arms, around
your bulging tear filled
cask
un-bothered by your
weathered wood
or tarnished rusted past.

And I say to you
No longer should you
shut this valve, nor
staunch the flow, but open
wide
so I can clearly see and not
to worry, you're not
invisible to me

I see your hidden tears
and its okay to irrigate
and let the roses grow.

* * * * * *

His tears fall on parched memories, like pouring summer rain -
thunder, lightening -
and the crashing - pain

* * * * * *

Lives Apart

Lives apart, worlds between.
Golden moments seldom seen.

Heartache over years gone by.
Changes never made, but cried.

Then upon angelic song.
Deep of soul forever long.

A glimpse of what, expected been.
Aches the heart and soul - no sheen.

For ever quiet truth be told.
Gripping terrible, life must hold.

Dust to dust, with time between.
Glimmer of hope for new awakenings seen.

But as it stands, it's just a dream.

* * * * * *

We've drifted too far apart - two rafts at sea - both may understand......... the ropes -
but without one...... the other ~~~~ just floats away.....

If I missed you... like the sun the sky - would you think me.... weak or strong -
would you miss my warmth.... or say goodbye

* * * * * *

I'll Just Stand Still

I'll just stand still
looking at the sun
and stare it down
until it lets me in.

I'll just stand still
surrounded by pages
wrapped tight
with curled edges
which explain the night.

I'll just stand still
until I see the glimmer
waiting for the stars
to explain my life.

From the morning
till the end of the sea
haze of the afternoon
as I watch the red skies.

I'll just stand still
and watch the night
until the blue eyes
of morning –
watch me.

* * * * * *

I walked a mind field..... every step I took.... to you – I feared....for my life;
but without you, I have no life – and nothing to fear

I've lost my ground - a quiet sorrow, beneath my heart - has yet been found

Upon my mind...... tied in bow - a string reminds me...... of those I knew -
from a long...... long time – ago

Take my hand..... and walk with me – show me all the stones we've overturned – all the leaves we've seen – just love me... holding hands

How can I listen - when you do not speak - or bear your silence - when I cannot bear.... the depth - of my own

With each whispered word - you breathe live.... into me

I love the morning dawn..... it makes me want to kiss you – so close your eyes – you are my ground.... and I.... your morning dew

Touch a star with your hand and I'll touch the sky with my love......
we are never more apart, than a hands width...

* * * * * *

Summer's Rain

Your ripened lips
drench me,
like a summer's rain
and the cherries blossom
on the youth of limbs.

Can you feel the weight
of the burning sun
as the purple lilacs sway
and the golden hair of wheat
makes love –
to the fields.

* * * * * *

And in the quiet of the storm – his youth….. disappears……

You stroke your words to pierce me….. like a silver bullet – yet I am no wolf – and you are…… no virgin

In winter, we'll dance on white fields, in summer, those which are green with envy; in-between, we'll dance to our hearts content

I am a dreamer – I watch the stars…. and croon…. to the moon – I am the tree…. by the river

I embrace her……. as if she were….. my loves dream

She walked me down this road, a lane with an end; trapped - she captured my melancholy……… then my hand

* * * * * *

Mind-fields

I walk through mind-fields
with a gentle foot here
but never there.

Terrified to see
what has happened
and what may be -
it's the uncertainties.

Each forward step my last
or two steps backwards
and there I am
standing in my past.

These little rusted signs
unheeded shots and warnings
hidden beneath tall grass
waving trepidation
which holds me fast.

I watched them walk
...no fields of view
then dogs would bark
- and I did too.

Deep in a mind-field
standing
listening
waiting
for the dogs to come
unsure of what to do.

Close my Eyes and Breathe

Through the door and up the stairs
I wander through the halls
afraid to knock
so I whisper to the souls
- who stare.

At the end, I see a room
an open threshold
just within my view
with a dim light
and a shadow
which I....
must step through.

Deep of breath
with warmly painted walls
latex coated taste
now dry of throat
heart beating
in a deepened haste.

Too afraid to move -
I stand
and listen... as the silence
grows
loud upon my heart
afraid - the bells will toll.

One large step
committed - on a hard
chair

I now sit
with slated back
too straight
within my eyes, I wait
and peek around to see
it's only me.

So I close my eyes
and breathe.

Pale Edges

Play me
Like worn keys on a piano

Fingers dancing on ivory skin
Bruised, beyond a note.

Artist Unknown

Water to the shore
Lapping at my pale edges
Fragile is my soul, which ebbs away

Resolute, the piper plays - a lament
But there's nothing left to say
Nothing left to give, but blood
Red are my tears, this day.

Dripping past pale edges
I simply wish, to fade away.

* * * * * *

In forest damp of hair, despair of mulch, a mindful floor with rotten leaves; walked upon, I'm left to stir - on this life's breeze

*No longer could I find my way - I was afraid to open up.......
afraid.... of what I'd see*

She looks at me with naked eyes - and I - return the stare

* * * * * *

* * * * * *

This blank page stares at me - a stark reality_____ with an edge

The mirror on the wall, captured life,
which rambled past -
now shattered.... are the pieces –
nothing more than .... glass

Her eyes - a mirror of reflection - a connection, between the two of us

Why do you whisper – these words I cannot hear –
and then you play with subtleties –
a pantomime... which your hands – make clear

Can you love me.... and caress me - like the sand loves...... and caresses.... the shore

Her heart....is where I'll live – or die

Don't say a word – just breathe – so I can hear..... you live

When is the moment..... that she changes me – is it her touch......
or with a word

Do the stars of heaven..... shine for me; as does the smile..... upon
my tired face – shine.... when I dream of you

Velvet are the hands which sooth – the coarseness... of an aching
life – and tender are the lips that kiss – removing all the pains

* * * * * *

"No Longer Does He Care"

He swims beneath a sea
wounds buried in the salt
fighting for humanity
a judgment of default.

Now parched is death
cracked beneath skin
his laughter hoarse
falters the banality of sins.

These are the harsh
realities
which bay behind the eyes
as dreams are washed
away
on drenched tongues
and flaming throats…

Acid bile, which chokes
words slurred
to sputtered thoughts
soon to be a ragged flag

strewn on this soured
floor
a door slammed
no saving grace
no coat to shelter
lost is face.

Pipes which clatter
hot bags of air
the only skirts which
flutter
are the open drapes
blowing with despair.

Heels dragged
bagged and tagged
the finalities are at an end.

No longer does he care.
_____

*See Authors Note 8

* * * * * *

Surrendered to the animal, of human life; a priced paid, with the daggered blood of morals - and ethics laid

But every love comes with pain ~ each soul is different ~ not everyone's the same ~ what victories, have been lost

* * * * * *

She Drank Time

She drank time .... until it was cold
guzzled it down her throat until
the doors closed to her unhinged mind
then swayed back and forth, to squeaks
of chains, dragging across dirt floors
which bound her, all the same
to steel post, rooted deep - to untold life.
She drank time, till the clock ran out
no chimes to ring, no song sung
desperate twisted thoughts unwrung
she thought that's when life began
soaked - in dreaded fright
shaking out, lost dim lights
sparkled eyes, now gone
arms wrapped tight
to lost alleys...
in the dead
of -----
night .

* * * * * *

I've lost my ground - a quiet sorrow, beneath my heart - has yet been found

Memories wrapped in cloth...an illusion-----still here; the more I search —— the more I disappear....

A teardrop fades, into the fabric wrapped around –
as cold seeps through his shawl of skin...
to shiver deep beneath - and within

* * * * * *

Sweet Reverie

Reverie with glittering lights
shimmering turquoise,
blazers…. finesse, and pink of night.

Cognac drenched lips
sweet whispers of Havana
with hand rolled tips, leaving
swirls of Hemingway in the air.

Succulent dreams
taste between golden seams
these delectable treats
with the Cuban beats…
trumpet his Armstrong Jazz.

Comfortable, in his sweet reverie.

* * * * * *

She sang in keys, which reminded me, of the colour in the notes; an angel in the emerald green, a rainbow in the middle of the sea

A wooden stage, stood bare, naked…___; the oboe played, on heavy notes - a weighted heart, despaired - as the curtains fell…… they wept

* * * * * *

The Darkness Doesn't Know

The deeper, that I go
the darkness doesn't know
nor hide my eyes.

I realize
I'm beyond my depth
just another drowning man
inept, with realizations
caught between her cries.

Rapidly I blink, and stand
stillness, gasping...
as I recall, the breath
of her scented lies.

All the while
I'm drinking in, this frothy air
which I now despise.

Waist deep
in the constant shifting sands
quietly forgetting,
who I am.

The deeper, that I go
the darkness doesn't know
nor hide my eyes.

On Top of Tall

If I stood on top of tall,
throwing life into the wind,
would I be carried off to sea,
left scattered amongst the squalls.

Would I be washed and cleansed,
or set sail beyond the curvature -
of the lens; no mast to carry me,
nor sails full or free.

If I stood on top of tall,
beyond a stretch to see,
balanced on the edge,
willing it to fall; would I then be
looking past and beyond it all.

Left standing, a finger to the wind,
a current of the time, everything in
view, and everything is mine.
The only thing I need to do -
is to stand on top of tall.

* * * * * *

The deeper I dig, the more...... grave... it becomes

*Cold coffee in a measured cup - grains of life displayed - so a gypsy
with a tattered mind, explains - why the stars fade away*

* * * * * *

Violin Strings

Violin strings, unsure what she'll say
tightly strung bows, wrapped in fingers
dragged... across scalp
Screaming Notes, made from hair.

Four strings tuned - to a fifth
holding bridge, till tensions part
and vibrating sound - echoes
singing, unwound starts
the opera walls cry, as
fingerboards pressed...deep
changing pitch......

On your feet, you stand
with buckled knees, which clang
the sounding post, digs deep
in "F" holes, that scream away
supporting bridge, as flying tails
whip about, and waggled chins...sag.

Violin strings - die away.....
freeing hands stop their play
a quiet sound, fades----...
until a teardrop - quivering
lands upon

- the stage.

She Played Too Long

She bides her time
at her will
knowing,
I sit beneath her sill
Waiting, waiting -
waiting…
always still.

Games of minds
fun to play
when other side, has no
say.

So smart of her
whimsical and play
never thinking
damage of delay.

She bides her time
at her will
knowing, I sit beneath her
sill
crushing hearts
piece by piece

I fall apart.
So smart of her
or so she thinks
not realising of
the heart she sinks.

I've sat so long
my love is numb
the game she played too
long.

I look about and see the
sun,
and stand to stretch away
the pain within my heart
because of her
those thoughtless ways
I simply walk away
and part.

She played too long
and now she's broke my
heart.

* * * * * *

He caught the wind between his teeth...... and shuttered~~~~~ in disbelief -
a taste of thoughts he'd chewed on...... so very long - ago

Did she see me...... wince - with each drop, the pin descends-------
into the silence......
of her - which pierces me - within

In the hollow of his mind — he found the passion.... he had lost —
over time

She is my willow — my weeping tree — long arms, she wraps around — holds me...
to her shadowed song

My words pale to her ink — a rich darkness, which she embeds_____ between these lines...... I have now read

I want to take you..... home — into my arms

Circle me — — take your hands.... and embrace me — draw me in —
and tell me who I am — to you

Breathe me in — like the white page..... breathes in... the ink — then grasp me — like the writer — grasp the pen

I'm yours — if you want me....... Take me — take me now.... like the night takes the sky — and I will.... be yours

* * * * * *

Residual Goodbyes

His thoughts lounge upon his day
with feet up - resting….
sunken deep into the grey - of mind.

A familiar comfort
with the unfamiliarity - of time.

Hands dragged through layers
as his watchful eye -~- ticks…away
an unconscious act, of a nervous cat
twitches, to a face at play.

The neuron scurries……
across the cluttered floor
a nervous jump, to a startled door
and the edge of seat…. - sinks.

He stands - unsure of why
to bruised aches, of memories
a deep breath - a sigh
of these….. residual
goodbyes.

I Hear A Bird That Whispers

This little heart which cries
to each beat upon a quiet storm
a tear drips, from withered high.

Her feathers wrapped
she cuddles to her breast
while others stand aloft
chirping - unconcerned
about her solitude
or the salty dew
in the mornings nest.

But far away - I hear
a broken heart which patters
and a little bird that cries
I hear a bird that whispers
and a little pieces of me…. just dies.

Delicate, my songbird
she matters more to me
then all the other birds
who simply fly…. on by.

No longer do I wish to
hear
the whispers or the tears
I want to look towards the
sky
so I can see my little bird
now flying……way up
high.

When you finally see the
blue
the sun inside will shine
and then my little
songbird
- so will I

* * * * * *

Out of a dream she spoke to me –
and on the wind.... I heard her cry –
goodbye

Can you not see the end of time - it's when you rest your head -
and I whisper to you - goodbye......

Her mouth whispers, drawing lines across his vision –
vertical blinds, erected –
falling to his vertigo...... mind

With a broom I sweep the night, so dust may fly around; in the
dawn all I wish to see– are particles of hope...through the light of
me

A tired bird sings, a lonely song for two; huddled in a nest –
the trees left to wonder –
would it make a difference..... if she knew

If it were night –
I would scream to you my passion –
the brightness of the stars and moon –
then ravish you... until the mornings light

I am incomplete –
a stork without a baby –
a tree without leaves –
rapids without a stream –
without you, I am only left - with me

* * * * * *

Mornings Dawn

Each mornings dawn
I search, while listening -
to the pattered beat.

My racing heart
which drums…. …. ….
and seeks.

For a glimpse, just a peek
of you.

This ache, I understand
pain, without a jab
ribs, which take my breath away
a thumb to plug the dyke
and wash me -
with your gentle hands.

I want to wake
each mornings dawn
knowing that you're there
not gone.

The brightness of my life
is dim -
without you, I have
no mornings dawn.

May Bloom

Once upon a time, I stood so tall
but now I often - well, sometimes
I fall, and wither to the ground.
I never used to be like this
all dried and twisted in my thoughts.

There were goals and rainbows
which never seemed to end....

but then, the colours of my life
began to bend - and twirl
....around the moon.

When I was just a boy
at the window, in my room
it all seemed so fun back then
until a shadow passed in gloom.

Did I ever mention
that I once stood so tall
I thought I had it all.

I used to think, if she -
would only hold my hand
wouldn't life be grand.

I'm pretty sure
I'd be standing tall - then
like a flowered stalk
and her the sun.

Well, I'll just sit here for a while
perhaps I'll make a castle
and gather all my thoughts
in a court yard - where all
my dreams
May bloom.

* * * * * *
I can see your flesh – the freshness of your skin – the delicate of you…. within – I see you – all I need to see….. is you
* * * * * *

Daniel Hughes ©
www.danielhughes.ca

The Light Shines

The Light shines on my window,
with each waking day.

Yet my nights are scarred by memories,
but who am I to say.

Dust has settled, and my eyes have cleared,
its the fog that worries,
as it rolls in near.

The spray splashes,
as dawn appears.

When my eyes open,
the light removes the fears.

The light shines on my window,
but the night is near.

The dust has settled,
but it's still not clear.
Who is far, and who is near.

Each waking day, the dawn appears,
Let it wash away those midnight fears.

As the light shines upon my window.

* * * * * *

She stood in silence…. watching me from miles away; scared to move - I was afraid to blink, fearing… she would fade away

In the dim light, he sat…. and watched the day go by - with each streak of light…… he wondered - why.

But as the stars appeared…… he knew his course was right - like the trails of his life, he watched - as they floated through the night.

* * * * * *

Snarled

Deep beneath the forest floor
under trampled rotted leafs
- of a fallen life.

Tucked between the "snarled" lips
lays the roots of man and tree.

Sits a scratching post…
surround by gnarled bones
- of memories.

Where the jackal waits
- nocturnally
- in me.

* * * * * *

I played…… the leading man – in this drama….. of the flesh

I stood poised – like a marbled sculptured statuette – as she ran her hands………. over me

* * * * * *

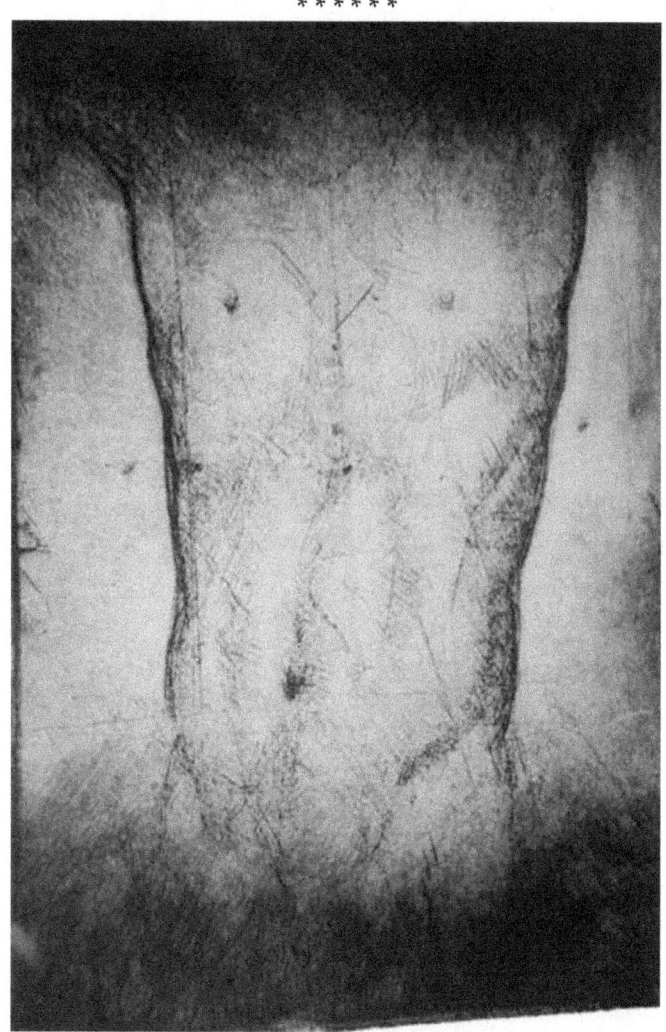

Daniel Hughes ©
www.danielhughes.ca

She Drew A Circle

She drew a circle upon her arm -
a closed and thoughtful mind within.

A tunnel view or a mind askew?

To breach the walls to enter the realm - deep within the circle, to reach the helm.

A fortress mind, of thought and skill

Years of living, tight within.
Always searching - where to begin.

Circle the wagons, circle the thoughts.

No one enters, no one leaves
she is left, but does she grieve?

When the circle closes,
does it lock everyone out, or
does it lock her in - only to spin - only to shout.

Do we stand off to the side,
always willing to abide.

Her thoughtless ways,
not meant to harm,
not meant to charm.

To breach the walls we try and try -
only left to sit and cry; she knows not why.

She only cares for thoughts within.

If I walk away today, will she circle the wagons, and circle her thoughts.

Will she justify, as have and have knot's.

Will she care, or will she wave.

Will she open her circle,
and willing to save.

Not just her, but me the brave.

I can only breech the walls so far -
then I tumble - then I scar.

Close your mind, or close your will -
I fear it's you, who will end - by sitting still.

She drew a circle upon her arm -
a closed and thoughtful mind within.

I hope she sees the wisdom

I hope she lets me in.

* * * * * *

What is your name to me... but sadness – my tears like rain…they pour – I am but a hollow man – when you are gone – I am nothing more

She looked within my eyes…… and caught an inner glimpse, which I never meant to show. I'm looking back…… now unsure, of where to go

Dark wind rushes to a forest, which looms - as branches lean towards the shadowed moon - and leaves whispers … in the night

I taste each word and feel her tongue - like memories in the dark of another world - wrapping each shadow, to hide our night - we tangle in the oils, which drip - caressing her, she is my light.

If I were the wind ~~~~~ I would only whisper…. to you

The reality of her….. is but a dream – a fathom… far too deep – I fear to pull beyond the seams – for it is I…. that will be the wreck

She is that love – those eyes…. which I crave – and tender lips – she is the apple on the tree – and my forbidden hearts….. desire

My thoughts…. are deeply buried within your flesh – and your flesh….devours these ideas

Her words, are but a wish….. and his – a sigh

You feed my palate…. with this art, you've made of morsels… these luscious words – which I now taste…. and breathe

* * * * * *

Magical Mind of Mine

Oh Magical mind of mine
It dances and sways to its own mystical ways
Oh magical mind of mine.

Many days its straight and narrow
others, like a swooping sparrow
spins and turns, with many thoughts
drastic highs, and lows to die
this magical mind of mine.

Why can't you see, what's inside of me
not what's lost on the sea of me
don't focus on this mind you see
but the bigger part of all of me.

Oh, this magical mind of mine
this wonderful mystical sea of me
my mind is only part of me.

This magical mystical fraction you see.

This magical mind of mine.

---

*See Authors Note 9

* * * * * *

Save him, from the dark of self - as the sun begins to set…..and a shadow settles …. on the hemisphere, of his frontal left

He spins web's…….in a circled mind; night till day - around and round - Caught…. Tangled…. but never found

I sail a sea of the mind, deep and wide, blowing winds, and rushing tides, the beauty of the calm, with tearful storms inside

I savour her – like sweet dew….. upon the morning grass - she is my daily drink – of life

Imagine your paper…… as the sea – your pen the sail – your mind ~~~ the wind – then imagine……… your love – is me

* * * * * *

His Mind

His mind was up….
Spinning round and round
but it went nowhere;
like circles of the day
which spun into the night.

A single thought
cast in a straight line
dancing in the mind
bouncing off a mirror
then caught -
in the vortex of a twirling

ceiling fan….. and time.
Like particles shown
in sputtered light
free floating…..
until the clouds come
which stifle the darkness
hiding - the moonlight.

He watches the fan turn
spinning around in time
but, with every turn…..
the clock slows
but never does - his mind.

On the Brink

A margin
along the ledge
of a land....
which verges
then converges
when a catastrophe
occurs.

But then...
I reached a point
a state beyond a state
to find...
no helping hand
which could abide.

So here I stand
this crucial ledge
steep along....
my borders edge
drinking, in the view
as I watch.... me spin
this inner vertigo - askew.

Do I cross the border
fall or stand...
on the brink
of this helpless land.

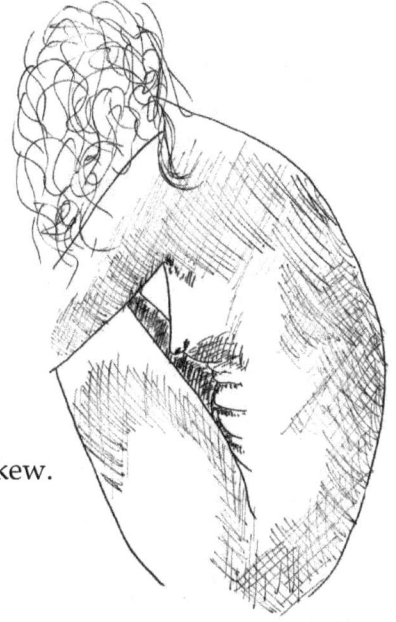

* * * * * *

*She pulls me in - spinning me around.... like a vortex –
dizzy and confused - passion and madness - often, one and the
same*

*A single line ----- in a fantasies dream –
or a reality entwined ~~~~ within the seams*

*Spinning Life...... capturing thoughts –
trapped between a mindful web -
left hanging_____ by a thread*

*If I stood on top of tall, throwing life into the wind, would I be
carried off to sea, or left scattered amongst the squalls*

*In a life of friends, you are the only one - I see you're parched.... so
I offer you....me - to quench your inner soul...*

*He unravels...... his thoughts – in the hope of seeing an end – but
he finds, that he cannot see around the bend*

*His mind dances....and twirls - to an inner song...he hears;
despite the difference of his years - he is just ... a little boy*

*Gouged into his soul, are dreams - a deepness of a life unseen; her
love penetrates, well beneath...those shattered.... memories*

Is he the willow - and does.........the tree bend - to him

*She ploughs my heart – with sadness deep –
while planting seeds of hope... which never grow*

* * * * * *

The Scattered Mind

Scattered mind, or
soulful searching

Seeing dreams, that
others misinterpret

Encapsulated within a
space, looking through a
door to life; the street
beyond is full.

We sit we chat,
the questions come,
the answers
circumnavigate.

The course never straight,
and answers well beyond
the norm.

To see within the mind he
sees, a mystery to me.

Yet a light begins to
glimmer,
as I begin to hear –
and appreciate
the moments we share.

The mind it jumps from
space to space –
as shining things appear.

A twinkle in the eye, I
finally see –
of a mind, not necessarily
unlike me.

The brilliance is the
dream,
the possibilities unbound

The course may never be
straight, but the vision
always clear

It's my friend you see,
who looks about and
smiles
his eyes tell the story, but
never the tale beneath.

Pain and happiness
intertwine,
and this I must
understand

The tangled web, the
scattered mind –

Non-the-less a friend of
mine.

* * * * * *

Your heart is stained – with my conscious

He reached an end – a barricade of sorts – this great wall…. within his mind – and no longer….. could he climb these thoughts

Is my heart, your desire - do you crave my love, like the wood…… kindles the flame

* * * * * *

Feathers Float Away

Buckskins, scraped with bare-knuckle scrubs
a destroyed village - runs down…to the mud.

As water rushes, then overwhelms
the banks - along the shores
of destiny, lays the soil of men
and their worn cloths.

Their knees are skinned
and so are the bloody red hands
of the coats - like Custer's last stand.

In the black hills of the greasy lands
no bands play, but seven-beats
of an Indian drum - are heard.

The winds change and clouds reform
as the feathers - float away.

* * * * * *

*She dabbled in the dark, slipping fingers through the bark, of me -
until my thoughts, were peeled away - revealing, who I am*

*Slowly......... the shadow overwhelms him - as the darkness........
hides the truth*

* * * * * *

Unexpected Moments

What are the possibilities
when you reach out - and find
a hand, which fumbles....
into the warmth, of mine.

It's this simplicity
the very magic and the mystery
of little dreams, that saunter
such a wonder, that we find.

In a world, which turns around
life is so much closer
these unexpected moments
- are often found.

So regardless of the circumstance
whether a rainy, or a sun soaked day
an occurrence, or a happenstance
it's the warmth of finding rays
surprising sparkles, which shine
in the middle of our day.

* * * * * *

Skin so soft - lips of dreams - moments...... which could have been
- but lost

My emotions, a rough and tumble spit of land; until she reminded
me, of the vastness & the span; by a gentle touch, of her hand

What are moods, but strips of paint...that peel away....; yet it's
underneath, that you'll see... the real colour of you... and me

* * * * * *

Change Must Come

Travelled roads
these graveled feet have seen
deep layers, beneath....
the past - of where he's been.

Is a ridden track of steel
a cold line - yet defined
which pulls the weight
- he drags behind.

A shadow, of a long day
he pines away - this stretch of mind.

But change must come
around a cornered bend
to turn his thoughts away
from this metered road within.

* * * * * *

*A bumpy ride – on an uncertain road –
a mind that jiggles - tosses thoughts in air… and landing everywhere…*

*She can say a word… and change my life –
the difference of a breath*

*The passport to my heart….. you stamped –
time and time again; the journey of your travels…
and my torn roads - within*

*He projects himself, this old and weary soul - while he looks
within, for the deeper side - of him*

*Upstairs, between the ears - the daily grinding…… of the gears -
life shavings,,,,, falling off - clogging up the cogs*

*She took her hands and held me - infusing was the warmth… and
supple was my mind - now – I have no worries left to grind*

*Her feathers…. were in bloom – like a flower on the rise – until a
shadow passed – and there it sat – a darkness…. by her side*

Your lips are emotional – they quiver….. with each kiss

*Fresh springs, rippling over rocks– slim tall oaks, blushing…
under blue skies– as we kiss beneath their canopies– just you…
and I*

*You are my magnet – I am drawn to you….. and I cannot……
pull away*

* * * * * *

Steel Cogs

Emotions, like steel cogs
they appear invincible
spiked projections
to scare away
bad thoughts.

Always turning
grinding, churning the
remains into a liquid pulp
within my brain, and
wearing me down.

Steel cogs gnashing together
like a tight jaw at night
headache, sore teeth and gums
grinding away the molars of wisdom
to flat surfaces of
fractured desert plains
like my thoughts,
scattered on the wind,
no substance left to
hold them to the surface.

Each spiked cog,
digging in, and engaging others
in a motion, which test the battle of wills.

They appear invincible	time after time
these emotions of mine	after…
but wearing down	time.
with each turn,	

For Me

In the darkness, I see swirls
little twirls of vision
which, spin around.

Interlocking webs of thought
fingers, that entwine.

Lightning in the distance
a streak across my eye
but when I open up
what do I see
but nothing.

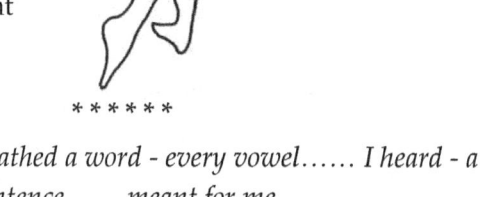

Sitting in the darkness
its only me that sees
these little twirls
of make belief
which are only meant
- for me.

* * * * * *

Silently...... she breathed a word - every vowel...... I heard - a sentence...... meant for me

Mental struggle always near - just to verbalize...... so others hear - Life behind some eyes we see - not always...... what we think - to be

In the light, I sense a part of day, unknown by the night - until the realization.... of the dawn

* * * * * *

Draw Me

Pull me like a direction
cause me to move
infuse me.... with you
an inherent source
like white lines of words
on a road of life.

Delineate me as a charcoaled vase
a portrait with broad strokes
this character you see.

Sketch a deep black window
without a shade
sketch the light of day
depict a scene of colours
unseen by the naked eye
hidden in the hues
drawn out - by you.

Reproduce, what no others see
and emphasize the vividness
an outline of a painting
washed out by the sun
a life between the lines

- then draw me.

* * * * * *

I am incomplete, a stork without a baby, a tree without leaves, rapids without a stream, without you, I am only left - with me

Her emotions, drawn on a canvas of him - like tears down a sullen cheek - paint, drips from her brush

* * * * * *

A Broken Heart

A broken heart
now split in two
no longer whole
these separate pieces
torn apart, by loves youth.

Like jagged edges
weeping, dripping…
mourning's due.

Which cascade
past the edge
of memories
licking shaded wounds
of discoloured hues.

Are the tender days
of silken youth
splayed upon an ageless
mind
then snatched away
unsown, by the thread of
time.

But as cold earth, dusts….
my furrowed brow
it's I, who still weeps
- for you.

———

*See Authors Note 10

* * * * * *

In misty eyes, of the morning sun, an innocents of a broken heart.... rises - to a setting moon

His tears fall on parched memories, like pouring summer rain - thunder, lightening - and the crashing - pain

Her love drips off me...... like a slow burning candle - easing down the sides...... of my life - as I enjoy each memory...

*Her feathers...... were in bloom – like a flower on the rise – until a shadow passed –
and there it sat – a darkness...... by her side*

He sits, he stares, he's unaware...... lost - inward is the pain - lost...... his stomach churns, lost... within - it's all the same

I am bound to her – tied in lust – what choice did we have – but to tear at our clothes.... in unison

I mourn for her – like a dust-sheeted man – in the silence........ of the room

* * * * * *

Nights Are Best To Crush Their Hearts

Hearts are best crushed late at night
When the soul and mind are at their weakest.

Set the course, slow and steady
Inch toward your final goal - show no pity.

Slip between the conscious mind
into the heart you'll find
A soft spot just below
Where feelings often grow.

Nestle deep, and wait your stay
Soon will come your vengeful day.

Light the spark, and spread the fear
Judgment day is near.

Pull the dagger, words go deep
Splay the soul, tears they'll weep.

Nights are best to crush their hearts
Just beware, as yours may part.

* * * * * *

I look at you..... like a wild flower.... looks up...... at the sun

I took her to the river – and I washed her….. in love

Our love…. is so deep – I not only kiss – but hold…. your hand

* * * * * *

* * * * * *

He drew a hand back - tossing the stone - and across the pond it
flew –
No ripple - no motion - The water~~~~
and his heart - - stood still

He dreams of cotton clouds, to wrap around his poets soul –
as he whispers to the winds –
and his love.... of sonnets told

I want to go to the river ~~~
just to sit and cry –
to feel the banks flood over –
uncaring –
forgetting, all the whys

With his broad brush and his elegant stroke.... across the canvas –
of her skin –
he paints her portrait –
and her cheeks flush..... with colour

I drink her in – and she..... refreshes me

Your thoughts.... envelope me – like the warmth.... of your body

You reside in me – you are my spirit

I am dismissed.... because my hair is grey –
but how can I be less –
when my spirit.... is so young

* * * * * *

Passion

Passion once ran through me
like wind in a valley
coursing through, now
hollow veins, these rivers
of hope -
now drained of dreams.

I rushed towards the
mountains high
to only find disdain.

Friends like trees
who wavered in the wind
and uncaring vanity
on crowed beaches of
cement
covered with icy stares.

I once knew passion
like the back of my hand
and felt love so deep
my knees would buckle
tears pouring on the
ground
- but it was never found
and I...left crawling away.

If you looked in my eyes
you would see deep pools
passions waterfalls
which drown me....

You would see love on the
beach - travelled hands....
that explore –
a mind that cries for you
you would see inner
strength
which carries you away
and you would see me
- holding you.

You would see my
passion
and we would devour life.

But life keeps trying to
devour me.

And everyone else...
- just looks the other way

uncaring... about the
passion
they just think...it's
another day.

But I try to find the
passion
- and you.

* * * * * *

*Feel the heat from my soul; dare you burn your hand, careful as
you rest, this passion, dripping.... between the two of us*

*Tears are going to fall, mixed with misty brine, this salty taste,
deep within my spine, still tingling - because of you*

* * * * * *

Just A Heartbeat Away

She cried in the garden
as ghosts appeared
watching shadows
buried under stone
of her life, which
disappeared.

Her light blue eyes
dripped sorry
unforgotten stains
of yesteryears
hiding her tears
in the rains… of
tomorrow.

Then she cried in a drawer
a journal of memories
of long heard footsteps
now turned the other way
fading….behind a closed
door.

One wall at a time
that crumbles away
shows the light
and a lover
who washes….
these shadows away.

Now she's my darling
in my river of veins
she lays next to me
just a heartbeat away.

* * * * * *

When he leaves, she'll fill his space - a breath, that doesn't matter - and a heartbeat… that's too far away - to be heard

I've lost my ground - a quiet sorrow, beneath my heart - has yet been found

* * * * * *

I Drank You In

I drank you in with my eyes
drunk upon your view
I tried to tell, but if you knew
solace in the silence
comfort in my blue.

My hope was cold
souls been sold
waiting for the price to pay.

Solace in the silence
mind so far away
but comfort in my blue.

I drank you in with my eyes
drunk upon your view
solace in the silence
comfort in the blue.

Sitting on the edge of life
bottle warm in hand
looking out to drink you in
solace in the silence
comfort in the blue.

comfort in the blue
bottle warm in hand
Sitting on the edge of life
looking out to you.

* * * * * *

Do not fade from me like the sun — nor grow old…. like the night

* * * * * *

******

Press me into you – like ink upon a page – and your lips....
will forever....... read my story

******

Drifting Away

She caught me on the tide
as I was drifting away
she was the undertow
who pulled at my will
while I tried to run
never from her
but from me every day.

Legs in the water
heart in the sand
struggling to breathe
until she held my hand
a safe haven
between the deep bay
and her promised land.

She moves me
gentle lapping
swaying my soul
until I was dislodged
uncurled were my toes.

Now in a stream
I'm tethered to her
soft eyes and a dream
no longer am I
.....drifting away.

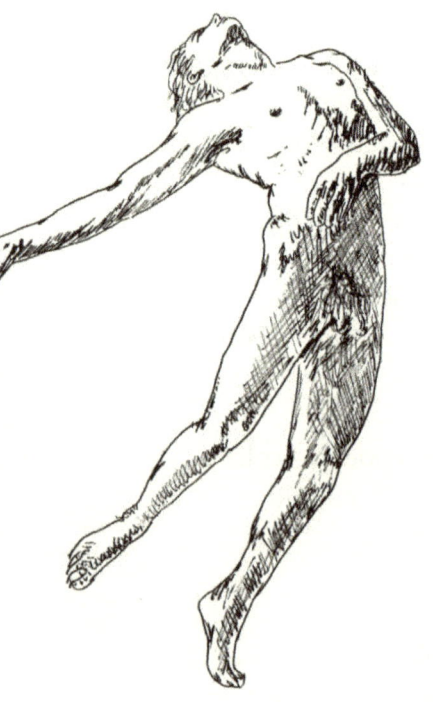

She Pulls Me

She pulls me like a tower rope
at the top of each hour gone by
each word spoken, claps a tone
then fades away - never says hello
or waves a kiss goodbye.

In my second life, I'll have an inner light
now....its two shades darker then the night.

I want a rose, without fickle thorns
no blood dripping in the morning rains
or burning pain, which sears my eyes
all scars left behind.

Coiled, deep inside - no longer will I go
what more could I give-up
when there's nothings left to hide
take what I have, or take nothing at all
take my loneliness - call me your fool
my loves yours, if you only knew - what to do.

No risks are free and no life is easy
when the sky falls, that's just the way it is
but you can always walk away
travel down that empty road and let your future go.

But I'm ready, if you pull me like a tower rope
let me hear your truth
just give me a chance and you'll be mine
back when time was young and our love grew
make me love you again, so I can hear the fading chimes
then forget the rope and just pull me to you.

I Wince

I wince, when I think of her sadness like a
throbbing pain of a deep sliver embedded
 within me, I quiver, shake with each ache
she feels.

 I endure her pain, with an intense fever, which
burns my very heart, singeing my passion and
blackens my mood.

I can't control it; this is how I feel. Her depth
within me, is so deep so entrenched, that I must
trudge through what crosses she must bear.

Do you understand this, can you feel this - my
passion of her despair. Can you see this love -
this love on a different level, beyond the years of life?
Can you even imagine…

Imagine my heart; imagine her pain of life, her
days of thought and breath. Now throw this ball
of unimaginable pain and fury into the air, let it
glow in its madness…

Let the fire from within her, build, bursting in tears.
This heavy ball, which is driven from her and into my
chest…, weighing upon my heart, burning into my
helpless being, my useless words - as they cannot
help her.

Then imagine how I feel, how I feel…how I feel.

I wince, because that is all I can do. I wince, because I want to feel her pain, I want to take it away... I want to take it all away.

If I could die on this day, knowing that she would be free for life - I would die... I would take all her pain, and wrap it in my arms, hold it as tight as I could, and suffer with a smile on my face.

Some may say, that is too much, who can bear such madness, such love, such passion. I say too little, too late; my job, my love for her, is to suffer, and hers is to love...and to love freely.

I want to wince, I need to wince; this is all I can offer her, I can only give her my heart, as my words have no real meaning, but my heart is for life - this life I can offer.

This life, I wince for her.

---
*Authors Note 11

* * * * * *

Her pain is of the flesh – and mine………... mine is of the soul

For her... I'll paint a smile – and for a little while - all those thoughts, those tears – will remain...on the inside

I feel her pain like a high note from the churches choir – and my tears now sing the blues

* * * * * *

Raining Room

Standing, in the middle,
of her raining room,
thoughts fall,
like droplets of life,
crashing to her floor.

A thunderous wave
these emotions, of
the moment and her day
as she is swept
into the sea...
and away.

On bent knees,
tumbling, in the breeze
of life, upon this very floor
... of strife.

Her sails set, full of wind
but dragging her
this life, has been.

As water flows,
beneath her,
soaked within the core,

lying in this puddle -
crying,
not willing anymore.

Shriveled,
dried and dead
tears upon tiers
piled too high to shed.

This woman of the ages
with smiling face above
drowning on the heels of
man,
while standing,
at the water's edge.

She puddles in her
thoughts
.... and life.

While standing in the rain,
instead

———

*Authors Note 12

Shoes That Walk

I put on my shoes, and they began to walk
Down a path, listening, while I mumbled and talked.

They never heard the rain, nor the splash,
they just continued to walk, and simply walked on past.

Flopping shoelaces, never tied in a knot,
Strings attached, like forget-me-knot's,

Always dancing to stay out of puddles,
Listening to the tune of me, as I walked about and muddled.

The soul bared the brunt, scraping the earth
Worn down by the salt and the girth.

Splitting seams, of these tightly worn shoes, tongues wagging, as if they knew - smiling in mirth.

Focused on the miles ahead, bent with arms swinging to an unsteady pace, unsure of my tread. I marched on as if in a race.

Reaching a peak, I sat on an edge, not sure what to do, so I looked down instead. And there I sat stuck, like some gum to my shoe.

Unsure what to do, I sat there and I thought about you.

The miles we've walked, now baring our soul, although a bit weathered from the heavy toll.

But, there's comfort in that, in these worn old shoes - who have seen it all, as we've walked, on these midnights strolls....

....and listening to these wonderful talks, in these shoes that walk.

* * * * * *

She wears me like an old shoe - a worn comfort to her soul

I never knew what to say - and each word....went astray; a different path - a different day

Her lips, rolled off me, like soft droplets...of passions rain

The pendulum swings, casting shadows below; he's left watching, as the mourning, lets the darkness - grow

With tender lips, he caresses you - press your back to him, so he may hold you - kiss your neck...and love you... and love you...

The silver lining...... a sailor said - laying on the ocean bed - was to see the whitecaps...... and feel the salty spray

Even if the sky fell — I'd tell her... it's the most beautiful of days - just so I can see her smile. Just before she says goodbye

Her mouth whispers, drawing lines across my vision - vertical blinds, erected... left falling, to her vertigo... and mine

She trapped my voice, an utter sound unheard - I told her everything... never a word, was said

She has a heart, without a string - nor rope to bind him: but she pulls on him_____ which makes him think

* * * * * *

What He Had Lost

Two wounded souls
on battles broken fields of hearts
- he bends to his sorrows end
and bleeds mercy, as she departs.

Oh such darkness when it comes
surrounds his shivers in the cold of blight
that he cries when his angels gone
for who will take him home... to you
when you're gone, to bury sorrows mourn.

But in the light of her reflective day
she returns to peel away - troubled thoughts
revealing life, beneath his scars of bark
to find a man she knew was there....
who's been too afraid to move.

So she placed a hand upon his heart
and held him to her ground
when removed, it was then that he had found
- what he had lost.

* * * * * *

The spirit of life, travels from soul to soul - and time is but a clock that turns - unaware of those..... who watch - as the wonders of the world fly by

Etched upon the landscape of my heart, is her soul - like a footprint imprinted in time... for all to see

* * * * * *

On This Side Of My Head

I was never close enough before its just as well, regardless of what you said. I knew you'd hurt me that's the way it is, on this side of my head.

All these blue skies, which disappear and the cloudy days ahead have you ever seen a storm just before the rain begins.

Have you ever kissed a stranger wishing you'd remember them
have you ever hugged the wind before the silence began, do you know what it's like on this side of my head.

Sometimes I forget my name other times I forget you and I are the same just don't wake me up, when you walk out my door close the curtains, then close my mind.

Have you ever seen a storm just before the rain begins I just can't do it anymore I knew you'd hurt me that's the way it is, on this side of my head.

That's just the way it is, on this side of my head.

Can I do it on my own anymore. I don't remember what you said but that's just the way it is, on this side of my head.

On this side of my head.

No I don't want to be alone anymore or watch the storms come in on this side of my head So can you take me, just the way I am knowing there's two sides to everyone.

That's just the way it is, on this side of my head.

* * * * * *

In the forest, between the pines, a path, to watch the twilight of the mind, slip across with little thought of time

I sail a sea of the mind, deep & wide, blowing winds, & rushing tides, the beauty of the calm, with tearful storms inside

* * * * * *

Call the Clan - For Me

On the peak I stand, to look about and see
this inverted undulation, now spreading out
all around - surrounding me.

Life is changing, the gravity, is liquid deep
a downward inclination - a flue,
which guides the clan to me.

United by a common trait, their mothers breast
once stroked; they return, this rearward motion
- a stairway down, to my pounding chest.

As the warmth flows from the sun
and river to the sea…
A mothers pride -

Call the clan - Call the clan….
they'll return to me.

Call the clan -
for me.

Written For Tomorrow

Who am I to count the cost
of all those loves I've lost.

Each broken pen and shattered page
of the poet, who pours a life
then drinks the pain
while displaced upon the stage.

He flails about and spits his ink
into a spittoon filled with paper
then cries his sorrow
as each word seeps....into the cracks
left dripping from the core...
- of his marrow.

Who am I to count the cost
of all those loves I've lost.

Who am I to count the cost
when no lost loves
have been written for tomorrow.

* * * * * *

In a shallow grave of mind, he buries his thoughts

Unfolding time - tucked away for years - I realize.....she never left, my mind

She retired to her mind, but my soul yearns, for her peace..., and refuge

* * * * * *

Deep Within

The brow creased deep,
seeds of doubt sewn within.

A tapestry of life woven
by hardship and by design.

Colourful threads intertwined
warped upon the walls of the soul.

A pictorial of life;
consisting of a distinctive character.
Rich and intense,
like deep purple, strewn against
an evening sky.

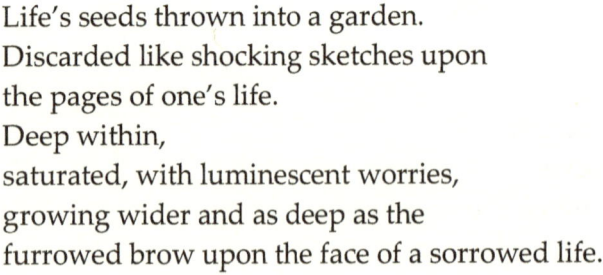

Life's seeds thrown into a garden.
Discarded like shocking sketches upon
the pages of one's life.
Deep within,
saturated, with luminescent worries,
growing wider and as deep as the
furrowed brow upon the face of a sorrowed life.

Deep within,
lays the heart of a lion,
a majestic soul, and
a painful past of worries
long held tight upon the
breast.

Deep within a tapestry of
life, held by a worn
threadbare mind.

Deep within, deep within

Deep within

A Mirrored Look

I looked up, to see him there
Not twenty-paces beyond my stare
Hidden in a crowd
With all the other blank faces.

Him blinking twice, was all it took
Drinking in, then shrinking from my look
I reached out, and I reeled him in
With a piercing stare and my glaring hook.

Wrapped around my little finger
He tangled in the air
I thought I'd wait…
and make him linger -
Just because he thought, that I would never find him,
while he was standing, looking in my stare.

A crying boy, with a withered grin
In the market, by the square
But twenty-paces looking on
That's where I saw him, just standing there.

In the window, with a glare
A little peek and a haunting stare
It was him - he was waiting
Hidden in a crowd
With all the other blank faces.
Just waiting for me…
to stare, into the pain of window
A mirrored look, he drew me in
With a piercing stare and my own
….glaring hook.

* * * * * *

She looks at me with naked eyes - and I, return the stare

Don't break her eyes.... with your shattered looks - a mirrored glimpse...as you walk..... by

Time between lives, when I open the door...to glimpse in the mirror, reflecting a face, while I lay down flat - deep in the floor

* * * * * *

The Soul Of A Child

The soul of a child makes the man
A weathered face and a steady hand
Words of wisdom from a generation
A father, a son, a grandson and on…..
An inspiration
A lifeline and a life-cycle
A generation past, a future infused with history
Was when all this began
A weathered face and a steady hand
The soul of the child makes the man

* * * * * *

Who can imagine - a child, who grows old… and life fraught… with life - a young mind, which withers of age - at the end of day

My fire out, the embers low…… many years ago - but when she came…… and sparked a flame - she rekindled…… my old banked soul

* * * * * *

Two-Cents Then

They laughed, ran, jumped and prospered
fortunate in the life and land they chose

Transparent pose, was Crystal Night,
World aghast, some seen fright.

Foreboding vision, future held
no one broke the horrid spell
Nations lost their heart, do tell

Windless podiums, uttering sounds
two-cent worth of expulsion, and repulsion

Political correctness, perhaps its start
Loss of nations, valued hearts

When they realised millions lost,
wasted time, deadly cost

Two-cents of words, by each nation then
equal four and six, then TEN

Grouped in numbers, strengthens men
should have spoken two-cents then.

———

*Authors Note 13

* * * * * *

I want to hold her as close as I can, never letting go; together we are one, apart, we are lost souls in the void between us

Can I count the cost of loves lost, or share in the treasure oh her love found

But every love comes with pain ~ each soul is different ~ not everyone's the same ~ what victories, have been lost.

* * * * * *

Ever Wonder

Did you ever wonder,
ever ask why,
ever just sit,
ever just cry.

That's what I do.
Then always wonder why.

Ever wonder,
if its them, or her,
or you.

Never looking,
not really caring,
so we say.
It's easier that way.

But deep and dark,
the bellows call,

sighing with the pain,
bouncing thoughts
off every wall
some even with disdain.

Did you ever wonder
… just once?

Did you
ever ask why,
ever just sit,
ever just………

That's what I do.

I no longer ask why.

I just sit and cry…

Afternoon Sail

Listless ~~ floating ~~
upon the sea... arms spread wide,
expressionless, that's me.

Driven, from the dock
into the pounding hail,
crashing waves, flat bottom dory bails,
water deep, knuckles white and cold,
piercing cries, cutting through wind...
blessed those, that live without sin,
upon the sheets of sails and the blue back fins

It's a splendid day, for an afternoon sail.

Slender mast, spars aghast, tearing sails,
which support the blast, from bone, chilling wind....
coming from up North – no whispering to be found on the
open deck of this vessel - sea bound.

Fat sails, men with buckets...Bail...bail - bail...
creaking decks, searing stout arms,
tearing muscle and limbs
blessed those, that live without sin
upon the oceans with the blue back fins

Black as night, 200-miles off the coast, waves galore,
smashing, pounding... sinking, thrashing peaks of white,
grasping men on sight
like a ghost ship, drifting...off to sleep, upon the ocean floor
so deep, no Savior's to be seen

Listless ~~ floating ~~
upon the sea……..
arms spread wide, expressionless,
that's me

Waiting, for the tides to take me home to my wife… and
family

It's a splendid day, for an afternoon sail,
with nothing but darkness, peacefully surrounding me,
and the now….. calm seas.

To Read and Deduce

She lies on my desk
and stares at me
so I introduce her
to an old friend.

Miss Blanc Page
may I introduce
this scoundrel
Mister Pen.

Dear Miss Page
the pleasure is mine
but if I may be so bold
can I press upon you
and engage your fibre
so we may further entwine.

Oh my Mister Pen
that's quite a line
but I've heard stories
about you, and you've left
quite a stain.

What a beautiful joining
that may produce
a young masterpiece
for the future minds
to read and deduce.

* * * * * *

I found you – no Jack, nor Jill – no pail or sea to swim – no strings…. or loneliness – just you – at the bottom… of my hill

Her voice…. is my landscape – and her vision….. my sea

Sailing in wild seas of emotions - afraid I'll run aground - to be shattered on shards of self - never to be found - again

The fog has lifted – and my vision…. now clear – yet I fear my ship has sailed – for I no-longer… see my love – standing on the pier

He took a pen and pierced his heart - and emotions….. began to flow - but now he cannot stop then - the river… overflows

Another dark day, where everything begins to fall; he drives a stick into the cog of mind, hoping to bind - his thoughts within

The gallows call, like a storm within - all senses are drenched - and the mooring slips…. from life

A torn map, from x to X - two kisses of a dream - a trek from the birth of morn - to the fading life of death

I am a child that never goes to sleep - a feisty beast of mind and thought - or perhaps… by a design and a twist of fate

Each day I rise - and hope to see the sun - it doesn't matter if it rains or not - it's the light within her eyes…. I want

My yearning, my yearning…. breathless, this battle done; a longing and a craving, for her, have I yet won - her prize of heart

* * * * * *

Flat And Simple

The earth was flat and simple
young, in heart and mind
perils but a book to read
not a thought of mind.

Swords were swung
games played [k]nights,
were shining still amongst
the quiet, peace and calm,
of the youthful thrilling
flames - of life.

The village of my heart
was Strong, built upon the
bones of youthful dreams
-
mortar, still spilling from
the seams

A story from days of old
not but 30-years ago, were
told - when the earth was
flat and simple and the
perils, nothing more - than
a chin, filled with
childhood pimples.

Far before the fanciful
dreams
when my [k]nights were
young and bold - of
fighting dragons and
dancing with fire
were the stories, wishing
to be told.

Now the [k]nights are
rusty, creaking from the
strain..., the misery
and.... the bloody rain.

Brick and mortar long
past gone, thatched roofs
pouring in - struggled to
maintain a withered
village of the heart,
now pumping, filled with
pain.

Peaceful are the [k]nights
no more - fanciful dreams,
now filled with gore - to
lay my head upon the
floor, and think... of when
the earth was flat and
simple - bringing calm to
the village of my heart,
and peace to my [k]nights
mind, when everything...
was flat and simple.

———

*Authors Note 14

* * * * * *

*She commands my heart - like a soldier.... on the field of battle -
and each word... loves cannon.... upon my chest*

* * * * * *

A Bell Rung

I draw my hand down,
upon the tower's rope,
a flicker of my eyes
a chime of hope.

Upon the bells ring,
upon the first note,
releasing thoughts
as the echo's float
down the sea of walls
bouncing through...
the hallowed halls.

Reverberating sounds
like a weighted crown
heavy in my throat
the words sinking, a
deathly
feeling, of growing bloat,
wrapping round the
corners
a moat between the castle
drowns.

Once rung, the twist of
fate, like a chickens neck
be wrung,
it cannot be undone.
The voice of chimes, have
struck a wall,
compressing, swinging
round to pummel me... is
all
swooshing back,
throughout the lanes -
hitting me, with
tremendous pains.

I draw my hand down,
upon the tower's rope,
now left to deal with all
the notes...the chimes,
which have left my mind.

Free floating, ever on the
winds of time, never
under my control or
thoughts again;
no longer mine....
these chimes.

* * * * * *

Too afraid to move - he stands and listens...   as the silence grows loud upon his heart - the bells begin to toll

The eleventh hour - strikes a chord, as hands watch time expand, and echoes of the bells are heard, as they toll towards - his end

Ropes pulled~~~~ two by hand - taunt of sound...... as bells are rung - signally, the bellows made by man

I fight her battles, within bare arms; surrounded by desire - I eventually bend to her will

With both hands on cheeks, she softly stares; a caress, which I'm aware - hold my head, to see my eyes...... and the love, that I show

In the darkness we sat, a twinkle in our sky - I turned to her and said - I love you more than ever, & more is bigger than the evening sky

She reminded me of the ocean; caressed and unabashed, I was wrapped in a thousand hands - of love

He feels left alone - a shell without an ocean... No press of ear, to hear the cries; she tosses him aside..... awash - in her tide

I'm a fish on a hook, with each look......she cast me; left reeling, as she pulls me .... too her

Seeking peace, he reaches out – to find a single branch – when he pulls it in-------- there is no other - hand

* * * * * *

A Heavy Chest

A heavy chest
I cannot breathe
with this weight
this weight on me.

So heavy, but you just
don't take the time to see
all these bricks
piling on top....

One, by one, by one... by one
heavier, with every single
crushing brick.
Every breath, I take – so thick

Air filled with straw and
mud
clogging me – each
breathe
a resounding thud.

Listen to the air expel,
what's left, is nothing
nothing left to tell.

You're crushing me
I cannot breathe
if I could only take a sip
a resuscitating moment
sucked between my lips.

A heavy chest, of bricks
on me...

Unwrapped is the Scarf

Creamy skin, with fingernail bites
red streaks obscurely sheered
absorbed in fabric, now glued
to a garment of a soul beneath.

No choice, but to wind then bind
enclosed within a folded scarf
arms wrapped to defend
these emotions over time.

But vague is the nameless pain
unexplained, in aimless rooms
intoxicated is the anguish
which squanders life
unable to reclaim.

Then windblown are the seeds when sewn
strewn amongst the traveled thoughts
unraveled are the disentangled threads
when put to bed to rest.

Unwrapped is the scarf
when love has passed the test
the nightingale sings away
the darkness of the shadowed night
while nestled in the bosom
as emotions, see the light.

Two Hands Make The Time

She makes me vulnerable
an unfamiliar feeling
which, I stumble through.

I reach for her, but nothings there
a disillusioned body
a void - - - of cold despair.

All I wanted, was direction
but I recognize her signs
and none - lead to me
so I'm left walking by myself
which she doesn't see.

What more can I do
but watch ------- and wait for you
as emotions. . . . . tick away
a nanosecond , or has an hour past
I'm left to dwell.

A sweeping hand---------------
which can change a life
but only if she understands
that two hands, make the time.

* * * * * *

I wrote her name..., and the paper, began to breathe

I can't breathe that brackish water, nor drink that stale air...from that putrid pond...of humanity - but if you ask me to - I'll try

Can you teach me – can you make me feel..... can you stop...this pain...from my teething love – can you help me breathe...again

* * * * * *

How Many Doors

What are you looking for
how many doors ...
have you knocked on
how many hearts –
have you broken
have you ever seen the paint chips
you've left laying on the floor
who am I to wonder this
or is it me you're looking for
or am I, just another door –
to knock on.

* * * * * *

Would you trap me – capture me – place me in your broken heart – would you hold me – love me - or tear me..... apart

Inconsistent impressions be, a falseness, of what we see; dangers of a broken heart, such failures, should never be

* * * * * *

You And Me

You confuse me
like a contradiction
with all your broken
words
half truths – that barely fill
a page
a language.... you've
discerned.

You make me....believe
then you take it all away
without a moral compass
you're unsure of your
direction
but to you – it's just a
game.

You hold my heart of
glass
all those....fragmented
pieces
each one a story – from
my past
and you forget -
that each broken shard –
is still... a little piece.... of
me.

You are a conundrum
a puzzle without a whole
no edges to define - and
I'm sorry – but you're
incomplete.

You are a friend – family
part of this domain
you are indeed...just you
with a little part – insane.

You see – I know who you
are
and you.... well – you
know me.

So know more games
no partial truths
no this.... or that...
just honesty between –

You.... and Me.

* * * * * *

An open door, to a torn mind, a shadow and a light; with a broken heart, he begins - to fall.... apart...

* * * * * *

They Grind Me

They grind me
like sand on dead skin
grating words of decay.
Spontaneous is the transformation
which rubs me the wrong way.
These hound-dogs
which hunt by scent
spoiling for a fight
beneath a sunny tree
spewing barks, that bay
at the collared man.
They grind me
like rich thoughts
crushing poor minds.
These turning cranks
of twisted, hobbled shoes
uninspired parities
and their insipid tunes.
They grind me
like a government
of cold pavement
which grinds away the street.

They grind me
on papered pulp
as the ink runs away.
Leaving but a worn soul
which has been ground
yet still…..
 they grind me.

* * * * * *

Could we sail~~~~ tonight – just you and me – and feel the crash of waves…. as we make love …… beneath the sparkle of the stars

* * * * * *

Sour Love

I didn't know
how to fall out of bed
everything she said
made my eyes drift away.

And I felt like a folded paper
that was read too many times
creased with all these edges
smudged....
with nothing left to say.

Now she tastes like sour love
red lips of wine and vinegar
poured.... into our bed of salt
she blames me
so she doesn't have to blame herself.

I didn't know
how to fall out of bed
everything she said
made my eyes drift away.

And I felt like a folded paper
that couldn't -
fly away.

* * * * * *

Am I a thread…… on my last strand – or a song….without a tune – am I in love with you – or am I…. just another man – to you

Heavy are these stones of thought….. which weigh…… upon my burdened head – her love….. is like a hat….. each feather…. made of lead

* * * * * *

If I Reached Out

If I reached out………
far beyond where my
heart touched
and just before my hand –
fell away
would I find you there
or would the cold air -
take my breath… away.

Could I balance time
two-lives – one past its
prime
could I lean on you…
like a drowning tree.

Can I sing with the choir
as we rock to the gospel…
can I meet John at the
station -
and shake his hand

is it the midnight train….
number 21
will that take me…. to
Galilee.

Did you hear the keys –
on the piano play
to dancing little
pachyderms'
did you hear the trumpets
- -
they too – will fade away.

If I reached out………
would you touch my hand
-
would you wave goodbye
would you hold me –
in your heart…

If I reached out.

You Are That Woman

Have you ever had a thought
a colour – that ravishes your mind
an all consuming happening
unbalancing – at the end---- of a line.

These dots, which don't connect
or lights that live…. only in the dark
and all these numbers – lined up in a row.

Teacher….can you see me now
I'm the worn chair –
who sits behind this desk
you can't see the logic
or see the tired tears
have you ever seen my face -
listened to my words.

When you watched me
I would watch the blue
just to change my mind
a comfort in the colour
unsure of what to do.

Then I found the pieces -
when I found you again
an explanation of my time
while I waited – to
understand.

An extraordinary person
who explains me – to me
no lies – nothing
undefined
just my tired world –
long since past suffering.

You are that woman -
who knows me
who never has to….
say a word.

Love Would Be Free

I waited for a long time
but she never came along
her heels, dragged the road
a deeper sign untold.

The trees whispered smoke
in the mornings dust
of the dawns second light
this sleeping menagerie
of a muddled mind
movements
- churning sifted time
on the days first breath.

Some days, are a long day
when your falling from the sky
some days are hard days
when lavender turns to purple
under the shadowed eyes.

I walked through the door
with life running still
then noticed, I was left behind
with no one else to blame
as the leaves fell to the floor
I felt them all - like fallen trees.

When I thought about it
what else could I believe
she once promised me
that love…..
would be free.

* * * * * *

Can she grasp meanings from the air - understand the letters, which make the words - or read the stains of ink, now mixed with tears

Plucking quills, bleeding ink...... dripping on a page; a headless dance of words - finally... they emerge

If sleep were a woman, I would surrender myself to her sweet charms – in the comfort of a longing night - and rest my eyes... upon her love

Imagine your paper...... as the sea – your pen the sail – your mind ~~~ the wind – then imagine...your love – is me

I no longer feel.... your lips..... drenched upon me – parched are these withered pains – that quiver~~~ in the hope of your loves rain

* * * * * *

Into My Tree

He is but a worn trunk –
she a vibrant lake…. which shimmers
underneath his tree.

A truth of buried roots
which hugs the desperate ground
is her love –
which binds me to this earth.

Each day I burrow deep
with gnarled limbs of thought
until I find the freshness –
offered at her stream.

I quiver in anticipation
as the tips of me –
reach out to her
absorbing all the moisture
and draw love – into my tree.

* * * * * *

I am a dreamer – I watch the stars…. and croon…. to the moon – I am the tree…. by the river

How can I not yearn for you – could you ask a sail – not to yearn…. for the wind

* * * * * *

Ink Stains and You

You stain my mind
like ink upon a crisp white page
where nothing else is visible –
or matters...... but you.

I see everything around
but it's black – then I see
the blue shadows
which surround...... all of you.

Then I put my pen down
and dry the tears away
I look at all the writing
that I've written –
but all I see......
is ink stains – and you.

* * * * * *

Ink pressing into page - a parchments thirst...is quenched - like grapes to wine - a divinity, this libation of the mind

Black clouds of ink written on a mornings sky - inspires the poet to dip the quill.... into the crimson hue, of heart and mind

Can she grasp meanings from the air - understand the letters, which make the words - or read the stains of ink, now mixed with tears

His fingers stained with ink ..... he draws upon the well - to find his muse

* * * * * *

Who Will Pick the Apples Now

Feet wide and deep of
breath
surveyed, with barreled
chest
is the taste of spring, now
a-buzz
on morning's breeze....

pink and white and
blossoms free -
listening to the bees,
which sing.

So succulent, the
memories taste
when a smiled tree is
born,
which bares the fruit
once naked were the
limbs.

How fresh, is the
harkened scent
returned upon... the
morning air -
of an Old Orchard's Inn.

But tired is the bark...
of sweat stained backs

who've tilled the lush...
between
basaltic ridges, in valley'd
fertile land.

Now arid is the creak of
porch and bones
as wild seeds of youth are
sown
upon the harvest
shadowed moons -
by the seeping dreams,
which flow.....
down to gnarled concrete
roots
just before the edge
- of a Halifax sea.

Rotten are the dreams
of old baskets, empty -
withered grey, without
sound
new generations...
stoop, searching - yet
unfound.

Who will pick the apples
now
- left laying on the
ground.

Can I

Can I say goodbye
if I roll my window down
Can I hold your hand
if I have no words
Can I show you pictures
of the life we had.

Can I touch your skin
or will my fingers... burn
Can I talk
or will your heart.... react
Can I hold you – once again
or will my tears – bring the rain.

Can I dream of you
Can I whisper to the silence
Can I think of you tomorrow
Can I just be –
your friend.

* * * * * *

Lay with me_____ entwine your soul with mine – wrap me in your very being – and I shall love you... forever – till the end of time

She calls to me..... like the wolf..... howls at the moon – and I bay to her.... like a hound... whose found the scent

* * * * * *

Just Beneath The Sun

I'm sailing away
with all these thoughts
a windy mind……
on a stormy day.

Did the sea of me…. change
when you stood
and never spoke a word
you just remained the same
but then you said you would.

You said you loved me
but can't reap what you sow
instead you…. tore me apart
like dark clouds – and the rain.

As I sail away, your soul –
invades my night
all this grey… which breaths the air
just fades my moon –
then fades away… the traces of you.

All these pieces – left in my mind
and they and I – miss you
so don't tear us…. apart
when the day is done
hold out your hand – and look for me
I'll be waiting –
just beneath the sun.

He withers in the storm
like a leaf on a narrow limb
holding dearly…. to her
he emotionally swings.
She cups him, in her gentle hands
just underneath his cheeks
eye to eye….she whispers
you're a precious leaf - to me.

What if the sky turned grey
what then… would you see
if the sun hid behind the stars
and the moon overshadowed me -
would flowers wither
and my beating heart….
fade away.

A Connection
A connection is the hand
that reaches out.
A calm touch -
to caress the mind.
The knowledge of life -
in a dark sky.
A shining light - of a friend.

Carry me across the ocean
carry me to you
lay me on a beach
without a rocky shore
then wash away my sand
and bury me …. in you.

He wakes up in a fog
and sips at his honeyed tea –
savouring this elixir – while she lays
in dreams of oiled limbs, shimmering – a pool where he dips
his thoughts, caressing…..an interior of whims.....

Don't come back to me
don't bring your gun
you can't run away
from all these dreams
they are all the same
just a long tunneled night
trapped in a tower
did the world change –
or only my view
as the old soldier, grew older
and his dreams
just faded away.....

When time has lost the time of day
and no sounds can be heard -
what is left to say.

When a withered leaf
falls from the tree
and no wind finds it way
then all that growth of youth
will be gone -
and no journey…..
will be made.

It's easy to lose people
they're never where you left them.

But why?

And then you're alone.

That's when reality hurts
and the mirror stares –
And you notice the room is bare
like the souls beneath your feet.

Every Whisper Is Heard

I hear the tin roof…. resound
in my broken home
two-drops past the buckets edge
and the rain flows –
to the lonely…… floor.

Clouds gathering
as the drums begin to beat
the wind…pining at my skins door.

Where is the sun
that burning pleasure
when her soft lips –
surrounded me
a battle I had one.

Wading through the water
looking for the door
I can't breathe
just the thought of her
drowns my heart… and me.

She's my echo
her love…. these beating sounds
my heart now trapped
in this hollow room
I listen to the tin roof
where every whisper….. is heard.

* * * * * *

I listen to the wind at night & hear her call my name - she is the moon, the stars & in the morning - she becomes... the butterfly

I am but a withered bean, who only wants to sprout. But if I could feel the earth – then I could feel the love – of the sun

* * * * * *

An Invisible Ghost

I feel invisible – a ghost
with chains…..
shackled to my feet –
or just another pocket
with too many holes.

But does it matter….
when you have nowhere to go
so I travelled to my mind
to look at all that history –
the riches and the gold
what else would I find.

Just another ghost
whose old and faded
when nothings real
that's just the way it feels.

Surrounded by life
as she passes me by
an invisible ghost
or just another fool
who's caught in a dream.

* * * * * *

I mourn her, like a ghost ship, lost at sea - tossed and turned, rusted, this empty shell... of me

You're not invisible to me - I see... your hidden tears

He measures time..... by the dance of clouds – these fragile wisps..... that kiss..... his eyes

She caresses me..... like the sun caresses.... a wild rose

* * * * * *

When I've Lost You

Where she's going, I've already been
so she can take that trouble
I have no more will –
to travel there again
and if you won't listen
then I'll see you off....
sure you'll say, I don't know today
but tomorrow – well....
I'll know my way –
and you.....
you'll be too far gone
and you won't see my tears
when I've lost you
and you've lost your way.

* * * * * *

She lost her love….. so many moods ago – but if I kiss her…… will her lips…. find their passion – again

If I can't be heard, then how can I be seen; if I call… out to you – and nothing… but the wind returns – then my voice…. is lost to you

He hides, watching pieces slip away – like sand, sifted through his tired hands, he slowly falls away… until there's nothing left…… inside

The shadow drips down the wall - to remind him…. of the length of day - and the darkness…. of his coming night

He barks at her, like a dog of war - with his vicious scowl of scorn - then he turns away… to hide his darkened tears

His breath is lost in the wind of words- as she takes away his lungs - then each piece of a torn breathless heart - disappears

What is flesh, if not the pains of love - that, which we crave - a single touch that starves our hunger

If you wish to hold me/ simply ask/ take your hand and guide me/ touch my feelings/ behind this hidden mask

Emotions – these violent waves – like a torn wreck upon the ocean floor – show the tattered remains…. of what was – now nothing more

* * * * * *

I Was Left To Listen

I gave her my hope
even when I had no strength
to wind the clock of time
and I was left to listen –
to her fade...... further away.

She would hide within the minutes
not a moment would –
or could she spare
just a second hand
a third wheel
nothing worth.... keeping
like a life without a beat –
left to fall apart
nothing left to give her
but a heart
at the end of a torn sleeve.

But I was left to listen
as she had no time of day
no seconds left...to say
or no time to give away.

I was left to listen
as she laughed between
those seconds
because all she said.....
was she had no time
and what she had –
she wouldn't waste
on me....

So I was left to listen
between the beats of time
in the hope that she would
hear
the ticking.....
of my forgotten sound.

* * * * * *

Torn between your mixed emotions - hanging by a thread - one desire...... the other dread

If I could hold you...... thighs to thighs - hinged between the time and eyes - Embers of your light of day - my darkness...... stripped away

* * * * * *

Back Home

A vacant lot
a piece of ground
within my soul
no path to lead me
nowhere to go
the question is
who will come
to save me
show me all the gates
that surround
and all the locks
to let me go
but who will plant the flower
to let the others know
that I was here
deep within this ground
but then I found a way –
back home.

What is Friendship

What is friendship
but a fragile flower
born from the earth
it sprouts towards the sun
but does it stand
when the darkness sets.

The colour of the petals
above the thorn
and below the leaf
a bounty of your heart
or red blood drips
a false rose, yet defined
which blooms to grief.

But your fragrance
is the perfect friend
such imperfections
that bend my life to you
this is my friendship
and the beauty of my colours
are for you.

* * * * * *

Like tiles, scattered on the ground - my heart, my breath, my soul..... exposed - for all around; this fragile mosaic sea.... of me

How can you forget the truth..... when tears have never lied – or driven home false words – when they are tied... to you

* * * * * *

* * * * * *

We grappled in a complex, an arena of our minds - until we found a moment - eye to eye - a friendship, which had grown - over time

We measured life, as our friendship grew; these years of brewing and steeping love - now this love.... taste of truth...... and you

If you wrote me a letter – would I smell the perfume; a fragrance of love – or the death........ of a tear

Call me your passion – drag me.... to your willing bed – kiss me with your hands, your mouth and mind... then we'll watch the candle burn

If you were the wind - I would be the leaves.... and sing you a song.....when you swept by

When you kiss me - you speak in tongues

She is an artist..... whose lips - paint me.... in detail

She bound me...to her - with threads of love; entwined, we felt this weary thrill, as we struggled...... to unwind

A beating drum...which echoes in the night – is your heart..... which calls me home

I watched, as each grain... ticked - - - by; whirling sands of time, now slowed - moments caught... on the reels of mind

* * * * * *

Time of Day

When time has lost the
time of day
and no sounds can be
heard -
what is left to say.

When a withered leaf
falls from the tree
and no wind finds it way
then all that growth of
youth
will be gone -
and no journey…..
will be made.

How Dangerous

How dangerous….. is
your mind
when you play with us
talking in circles
just so you can wrap me
up
with your long fork
tongue
it's a magicians rope
which I can't untie
and run away
from those red lips of
yours.

How dangerous… is your
mind
when you're serious
when you're bound to me
how dangerously sublime
when your serpent tongue
inspires me.

When it's four o'clock
and the streets are bare
the church bells are
ringing
that it's way past three
A.M.
but your tongue is still
telling me
all these stories
which make my hair stand
on end.

How dangerous… is your
mind
when you're serious
when you're bound to me
on a four post bed
will you tell me all your
lies
or will you talk in circles
instead.

* * * * * *

She is my demon – dangerous in every —way – a mischievous angel – she tortures me…. in my mind – she plays

* * * * * *

A Constellated Mesh

My thoughts are garbled
muddled in their concern
they have failed to find… connections
to feed…… the stream of mind.

But if I walk….. away
will they ever find – those words
which fit between the lines
and help me see……

the light before the grey.
So now I sit ~~~~ tangled in this chair
a constellated mesh….. of disconnected dots
like little grains of sand – without a pearl
or a man….. lost in moments
thoughts…… which cannot stand.

* * * * * *

Your love is seamless – when sewn into me…~~~~~~ the very fabric of who you are – is what makes the tapestry – of me

Words – lingering unheard – these lonely stars, which never see the butterflies – or hearts, which never feel the pain – of lovers words

* * * * * *

Once More

Old words, which you once read
left scattered on the floor
now forgotten and upside down
just a book upon your shelf –
am I no more.

Perhaps I'm torn
tarnished at the edge
but I ask – is that not a sign
that I was once well read.

When we first met
you held me….
like a newborn leaf
just fallen from the tree.

You breathed me in
I was more than just a scent
dare I say –
I was once the very essence
and nothing less, nor more.

I'll wait…..
one day you'll see me sitting here –
your old friend
perhaps, I'll be propped against the door
you'll dust me off – invite me in
and you and I – will read together
once more.

******

You are the dragon, which my body trembles to – for your heated breath….. devours me – as the knight… chained in your wicked den

To say I "love" you – is but a small… inexpressive word – how can I express…. to the world – that "you"…. are my universe

******

I Want To Tumble

I want to tumble –
tumble through the dark of life
and spill into the light.

Then roll end…… over end
until I find my equilibrium
and stand balanced
between these two feet.

And then I want to plunge
headlong into this froth of life
and drink……
until my thirst is gone.

Then pour me into the sea
so I may float away
and the waves
can tumble…. me.

* * * * * *

I want to feel life – and that life begins.... in your arms

With each kiss.... her love - was emblazoned..... on my lips

Your words~~~~ flow to me – they drench me.... like rain drops – or they are the sun...... which illuminates....... my eyes

She descends on me.... like the moon - and I rise to her.....like the morning sun

I want to feel life – and that life begins.... in your arms

With each kiss.... her love - was emblazoned..... on my lips

She descends on me.... like the moon - and I rise to her.....like the morning sun

Watching clouds that dance - as they slip between the streams - how graceful, I imagine, and seamless - it all seems

Don't say a word – just breathe – so I can hear...... you live

But you are my heart – can you not feel that – then put your hand upon my chest.......... and feel me..... as every beat.... is for you

It's not what you say to me.... that hurts – but the unspoken words..... in your eyes

I stare, looking backwards... Looking at what was.... and where my dreams - were

* * * * * *

Away

We first met
in the darkness of night
I would hold her to me
strike a word
to light her
see the flicker
in her eyes
as the hardness
dripped away.

Now I watch her
this vision in my mind
a flicker of a candle
which over time –
melts away.

She was my light –
and now
that I can't see
I realize
that the wind of life
has taken her –
away.

* * * * * *

*Your words~~~~ flow to me – they drench me…. like rain drops –
or they are the sun…… which illuminates…… my eyes*

* * * * * *

* * * * * *

Walk with me – hold my hand – and then take me..... to your heart

You are.... a miracle to me – to touch you – is to bathe in love –
you are.... my Jordan River – and you've set my heart.... free

* * * * * *

Lake of Tears

He watches the rain pour in
as the black clouds
gather overhead.
Emotions thunder
sparks fly
and the siren by the lake
begins to sing.

A heart expelled
pierced by the shrill of air
as she smiles at him.

Call me home
allure me
take me there.

Run your fingers
through her golden hair
kiss her neck
her lips –
then drown me
by the lake of tears.

* * * * * *

I've sailed the seas – and watched the stars – but I've only dreamt….. of nights like ours – under…. your howling moon

There's no words – to describe you – only the flow…… of the silence – as I just…. Love – to watch you

When I look at you – my eyes just stop – and watch – it's only then…. that I realize – that all my fears of loneliness – have gone

You woke me…. from a sleep – where I was…. deep in your arms – now that I'm awake - touch me – and pin me….. to your skin

Bent in sorrow, while searching to be found - the firmly planted roots of ground - under a weeping willow - sitting quietly….. unfound

I long for you… like the mountain, which craves the sky; to reach for you…… and touch your skin of silk – and hear the breath of sighs

You are my garden….. and my desire – you are…. my English rose – when you strip away…. your thorns

Our thoughts entwine – like lovers….wrapped between pristine sheets – the purity…of souls

I seen the storm - it rose above me - so in the clouds I stood… to weather all the rain - until, they morning came

* * * * * *

To See The Bridges

I want to see the bridges
that span between
for you are
that savoured land
that only I can see.

To stretch to you
past these beams of hope
tossing girder'd thoughts behind
so they may fill the void
these years – of loneliness.

What shape
does our structure play
and all that lies between
obstacles of nothingness
except what we
may make believe.

I want to see the bridges
that span too far
so we can tear them down
and walk between
refreshing what we had
and joining
in what will be.

Deeper Than The Flesh

I don't know how it got this far
but my love is deeper than the flesh
 transparency, which I can't deny
or this lucidity, I see -
in the depth of your blue veins.

As I articulate my tongue
do you not feel the same
or is this a game of futility
and I'm, just misunderstood.

You are the one, who engages life
while I watch the wheels turn
then spin around three times
and hope the answers come.

I don't know how it got this far
but my love is deeper than the flesh
if this you understood
then the rest
you'd understand.

* * * * * *

I swing to you – like a door unhinged – on a ship~~~~ now lost at sea – wont you try to find me – on these waves… and take me away

My heart – is addicted….. to her

* * * * * *

His Last Breath

The lion sleeps
in the comfort of his heart
while the claws digest
in the belly of the beast.

Turmoil, twist and tears
now knotted is the mane
and the pride, long gone.

Where lays the open peace
the Savannah once held
these gentle windswept fields
where the golden hair of sun –
once lay.

No longer can his roar be heard
as the silence claims the day
and parched is the earth
where his tears fall between the cracks
never to be seen again.

He rests his head
and prays for death
he listens for the night to come
no longer does he wish to roar
but to hear the sweetness –
of his last breath.

* * * * * *

The sun.... has left his eyes – and draw down.... his face – to set upon.... his breast of life

He walks "down to a sunless sea" – to watch the drowning of the waves – to contemplate – or to wash away – his life

My heart sits.... at the bottom of the lake - waiting - - - for the sun..... to guide me
His mind bends to the sea.... as the waves cleanse his heart - and a sandy shore.... washes her.... away

The dog growls - as does the master - tired of the leash.... that binds them

* * * * * *

Freedom of the Sands

Do not bring your weight
to bear upon me
nor dig your soul
into the fibers of who I am'

If you allow me the
freedom of the sands
then I shall rise to you
and together
we shall walk
step by step
....
as one

In All The Faith

She lost faith in me
and lost the love of hope
rubbed her hands together
smoldering in this friction
a sudden clap –
to make me listen
to stay or maybe go away
waking past the fears
but unsure with all this doubt
left standing –
not knowing how she felt
drifting in the sea
where's the shelter
of your heart
don't let me fall apart
tell me where the faith is
so we can start –
again
forgetting all the rain
remembering all the fun
regaining all the faith
to just be you –
so I can just –
be me
and we can both
believe again –
in all the faith.

* * * * * *

Our legs entwine, like the morning sun embraces the sky – and the heat.... penetrates the passion of the earth

I love you today - I'll love you... twice as much tomorrow - and then I'll love you....again - until the end.... when I die

Your skin is my heaven, your breast my pulpit – let me kneel before you – and I shall pray to your divinity of soul

Look at me – enter my eyes – see within my soul – and tell me..... what you see.... in me

* * * * * *

What Tomorrow Brings

You are a stranger
who soaks my sheets
leaving me ingrained
with marks upon my back
and wrinkled thoughts of mind.

Now I sit on this ledge of life
feet dangling -
with these to's and fro's
as I am left to ponder
what tomorrow brings.

Hidden

You hide me -
in the recess of your mind
the furthest block
a box
as smooth as new.

But all the other ones I see
are chipped -
tossed about -
and opened many times.

Silk is my skin -
so thin am I
this smooth box
with a tarnished flap of mind.

I feel the weight of you
this crushing loss of breath
hoping that you'll see me
and open me to you -
or let me go.

No longer trapped
forgotten -
in this pristine place
hidden -
in the back of your mind.

The Blank Page

The blank page stares at him -
not he at it!

These raw fibers - exposed to life.

Filaments of nerves___ flinching
floating - tender... to touch.

An emotional clitoris
uncovered....

Hot is the blood, which runs beneath
shockingly cold - fingers.

Draw me in - infuse me
light my eyes, so I can see
tangle me in ~~~ in you
make me scream... till tears run.

Stain my pages
fold me - tear me
read me.

Hold me!

Fill me

with you....

Exposed

Open nerves
these raw emotions
tangled
and now exposed.

He had no shelter
no means to hide
stripped of all his layers…
his skin---- peeled away.

Now on display
he descended down
beneath the crust of air
his heart congealed
within the mess
of unconcealed despair.

While those who watch
- dissect him
piece by little piece
these exhibitionists
revealed
they see themselves -

exposed.

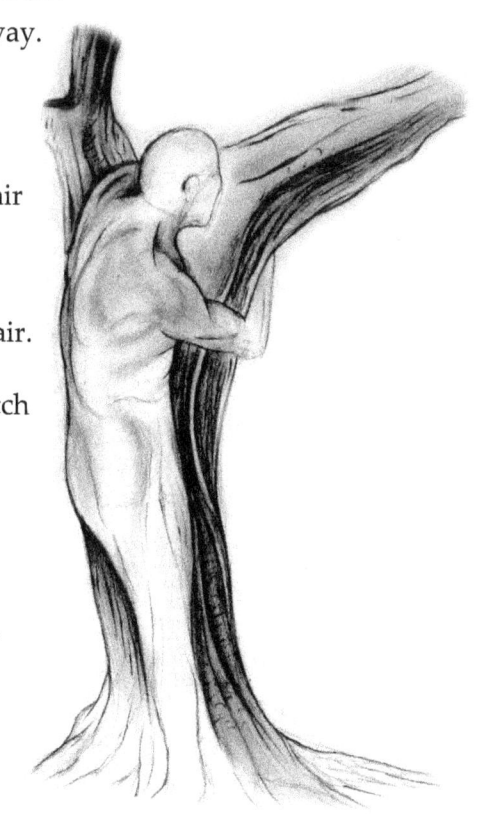

Beating Drum

One-hundred feet
trampled by….
to the aches
of the beating drum.

Their rhythm
called the souls
, which feel
the stoic virtue
and the thunder -
of the guns.

Fold the flags
dry the tears -
then stand at ease…

Hoist your drinks to them.

These boys, these men
the lads -
a hand upon my chest
I feel you there -
and ache
of the beating….. drum.

You Can Paint Me

When you drape your hands
across the canvas of my skin
can you feel the bristling -
of the brush?

Will you sense the tingling...
the passion of the paint?

Can you see the vision -
that you'll create?

Each stroke....you'll weave
like coloured fingers of thread
entwined in the tapestry of me.

You can paint me
in the dark
until the renaissance
of dawn
you're a master
of your skills
and I a sculpture.....
of your artistic will.

I Understand

I understand your tears
when drenched …
in sorrows rain.

I understand the deepness
of the furrowed mind
when tilled….
and the clank of thoughts
when struck against the
pain.

I understand your shallow
breaths
when I hear the
whispered beats.

I understand your cry
when lungs collapse
drawn-in by the ache.

I understand ….
when you don't
understand
yourself.

But you can understand
this -
a soft heart with a
shoulder
to rest your worries
and two strong hands
to caress away…..
your pain.

Is an understanding friend
regardless -
of the rain.

Feed The Fragments of Your Soul

I feel her hands, which strip my skin
unabashedly they slash at me
to peel away her thoughtlessness
looking for the profit in a pound of flesh.

What confessions can I make
while trapped in the quiet of this storm
as the serpent slithers, wrapping me in coils
~~~~ smiling… with those razor teeth
a magician - trying to reshape, not reform.

But I am only me - one single rooted soul
you can bite the apple
but you can't use me….
to feed the fragments - of your soul.

She Pushed Me

He cast his shadow
to see what he can reel
a splash of smoky shape
now, no shape at all.

Cold ice under foot
a steep hill without a
slope
she pushed me.

Please -
don't ever touch me
until you hear me fall.

Nurtures Life

Has the sun fallen
where shall it hide
and wait till dawn –
so it can choke
the impious
reminisce of night
and laugh
as the moon crawls away.

To see the sun
on a virgin sky
caressing
white clouds of breast
like the silk of mornings
dew
is a child sipping
on a new day –
as the mother
nurtures life.

Stars

How can I call to you
when all my words are silt
buried - underneath my heart
how can I feel
with everything
I've felt?

I'm too tired to shout
too hoarse.

Where were you
when I couldn't be found
too afraid to hear the thunder
when I lost my ground.

So when I'm on my own
don't squeeze me.

Hold me
take away the cold
stop me from crying
and bring me home.

I forget what I knew
but I knew I loved you.

Don't banish me
nor see my faults
don't take away my breath
for all I have .... are stars

and you.

In The Mist

She held me -
as if I belonged to her
nothing else existed
no wind, no trees -
no leaves.

A mountain
trapped between two valleys
a trickle and a stream
a place where dreams are held
captured - but unheard.

So precious is the sound
wrapped in rain
feelings…..
droplets, which began
like smooth morning jazz
a clarinet
closed eyes – and
dancing fingertips….
on my ivory skin.

Morning's tender lips
which kisses me
suspended -

in the mist…..

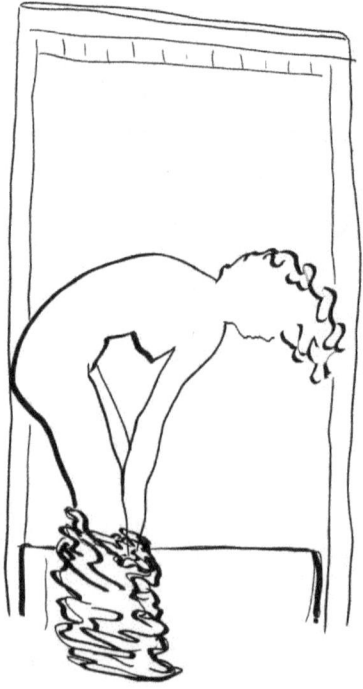

Whispers Love

Can you feel the breath of dawn
this sensuous whispered sigh,
which dissipates the clouds
and strokes the moaning hills.

Tender lips like feathered feet
snared drums
my heart beats…………..

Horizontal, till the golden mound
raging oaks-----pine…..
heaven parts
can you feel it now -
the breath of dawn
as the morning -
wakes.

Shivers
waves upon a lake
raging falls,
gasping at the earth
liberating senses
tastes the dew…..
as morning purrs.

Then feel the breath of dawn
as it whispers love -
to you.

I Hear

All I hear
is the cry of the trees
as they lean away
anchored in their beliefs.

We all watch
as their leaves – fall away
the earth screams
and the light fades
greens, purples, reds –
decay
a year is mulched away.

Life erodes
to only be enriched
eyes and heart blossom

all the stars – seek a new
day
all the broken limbs
sprout again
born upon the wind.

Now I hear
the Mockingbirds
and the soothing beauty
as a songbird nest.

Now I hear the life
which grows around
the trees.

And now I hear the life –
in me.

Atop The Pier

Your words bear a heavy tread
what else need you say -
that you haven't said.

Crushingly, my pillow fills with tears.
Who are you to brandish me
a torn flag who flutters in the wind
or a symbol burned upon the ground.

I may be lost, but no longer counting fears.

Carelessly you domineer
tethering me –
you tie my hands,
so I may never feel the truth - of you.

Dump me in the river – wash my years.

What fool I am to you
these outstretched arms
to catch your casting stones
my pockets may be full –
but no longer do I feel the weight of you.

I used to feel the water -
but now, I stand atop the pier.

Those Hues - of Blue

I first drew an image, to see if she was true
or was my hand influenced
by the renaissance
painted in the aftermath of hues.

What choice did I have...
but to dance... upon her ivory thighs
stark white keys, waiting to be played
soft music - high notes --- and sighs.

Tell me – is there a better way to paint
then with your fingers – and your eyes?

But she took--- liberties with me
and spilt my soul_____
until her brackish night was full.

Unsatisfied, she took my brush
in soft deep tones...of hush
she made me - the mistress... of her house
my fire, now burnt amongst the canvases -
of her un-kindled flames.

But how could I - a master painter
not find the light – deep within
to revitalize her darkest moods.

So with my palette in hand
I stroked her canvas
till I seen my wanting ways
then I painted her
and took away....
those hues - of blue.

The Show

Each Face a play
a twitch
a wrinkle
an actors line
a smile smuggled out
between the curtained
teeth
in this drama of the flesh.

But the fabric of life
this sadness which nags
like **BOLD** words
splashed on white walls
with patterned thoughts
now peeling away
to reveal –
imprisoned feet.

A face creaks
and the shadows hide
stage hands behind the
eyes
but the show…..
the show –
must go on.

Why Is The Water Still

I went to find her
down by the water's edge
just past the rushing brook
where an old tree never slept.

Stumbling over roots
now rusted to the shore
trying to find a way
trying to find the door –
trying to find…. her scent.

As the candle burns
to help the blind
I no longer see the sky
unsure what happened
when our life turned into time.

On the rocks… looking out to sea
she never turned….
but asked me –

Why is the water still?

Divisions

A short walk along a creviced wall
reminds me – of the sheer enormity
of the fractures beyond the seams
these divisions, which divide us all.

Coloured gaps – of paint and spackle
puttied joints of politics and bonds
heartbeats which flutter –
words – gavels without a sound.

Stop and listen – to the wind on hills
these trees with shallow roots
that topple down the streets
and homes, build upon the land
collapse – as the framework snaps.

Underneath the rubble sits
these barren stones of time
a painted picture – of humanity
forgotten lessons of our time.

What I'm Not

Can you feel
the depth of mercy
or fill the void.

Can you feel
your destiny
or the air.

Can you feel
this graveled earth
or only your despair.

Can you feel
my arms
or the solitude of peace.

Can you feel
the heavens
or your soul.

Can you feel
the fire
or struggles, which burn.

Can you feel
my hand
my heart
my soul
or understand.

Can you feel
the passion
or only –
what I'm not.

Only The Silence Remains

Are you the pillar
and I the earth
your vision to the sky
my solitude –
between the roots.

In discord – you chill me
what must I do, but heave
to reach your height of frost
while my heated thoughts
smolder by the fire.

What contentions
do our minds pretend to play
when your columns are so high
and my dissension –
a sentiment away.

Then what is left to say
when all the words have gone
and only –
the silence remains.

A Dot Upon A Page

I mean nothing to this world
that's just the stark reality
an insignificant truth.

Remove the stain of clothes
a costume if you will
and what you'll see –
is nothing.

A dot upon a page
A severe austerity
A blemish
An outrage.

Erase this speck
black soot
dust
and what's left
but the starkness –
of the page.

Un-Engaging Is The Sky

Un-engaging
is the sky.

Grey, white and Black.

The winds blow
to a howling laughter heard
as the clouds distort the sun –
And no smile is seen.

Hands to reach
which cover hidden eyes –
as the brightness
begins to fade.

Un-engaging
is the sky.

As the world revolves
to turn around and see
that love
is on the other side.

But un-engaging
is the one who cries –
when they have lost their smiles
regardless of the one who tries.

Un-engaging
is the sky.

Grey, white and Black.

As the wind fades away
to try another corner –
of the sky.

Abacus Mind

An Interesting thing – you and I
we wash emotions like dirty cloths
and hang them inside to dry.

We wrap them in a towel
tightly wrung tissues of our soul
then we watch them drip.

These un-drying tortures
leaving tears between the eyes
sliding thoughts from side to side
on our abacus minds.

An Interesting thing – you and I
one bares the soul
to dry the cloths
while the other one runs
hoping the wind –
will dry the tears.

Jukebox Eyes

Where are you
where have you gone
my ears can still taste –
the flavour…. of your lyrics.

These lost echoes
in a chapels steep
to the warmth of amber
in my 'mourning' tea.

Memories –
of old records play
in my jukebox eyes
as I still hear
the sound of you.

Even On The Darkest Nights

Nerves exposed
sleepless emotions
dead weight.......
on hollow rafters
which scrape the floor
then watch –
as all the little thoughts –
scurry.

Eyes closed
to watch the wind
who else can blow away
the clouds –
perhaps a friend
who can wrap around
their arms.

Openness
in these blue eyes
who knows the pain of days
but lucky are the stars
for they brighten you
even on the darkest nights.

A Set Of Stairs

A set of stairs
not one but two
some up
some down
but when I look around
I simply sat
to wonder all the souls –
who've tread……
and left a trail of creaks.

The weight of life
has worn us down
to a hollow middle plane
yet still…..
we jut our nose
so it can take the brunt.

Now on the landing we stand
on firmly solid ground
to pause a moment –
look up,
then down –
so we can choose
our path.

When The Pendulum Falls

Watching grey clouds
fold into wrinkled eyes
as minutes march
to the top of hours
while I stand by
yelling at the day.

Where did they go –
those unknowns'
moments over time…..
it's a different story now
as I've lost my kite
in the wispy wind of years.

And no amount of soul
can kiss the lips
when the pendulum falls
and the time –
turns into night.

Drenched

What a charade
is this feigning flesh
a pretense of the past
so deceptively deceived
are these memories.

Is what they're looking for
what they'll find
or a debased travesty
known within the mind –
of a brazen tasteless life
just a pantomime of
words
left filmed upon the
tongue.

What a charade
is this feigning flesh
a multitude of frauds
which leaves……
the rest us –
drenched.

Yesterday

Turning stones
shows the grit –
layers, beneath
the hardened skin
the underbelly
where life begins.

As emotions bound
from rock to rock
which bear witness –
to the imprints
within.

Mother earth
is this the sun
have the burdens
been undone –
will the sea wash away
the salty brine…..

of yesterday.

His Memories

His heart lies
beneath the stone
where freedom –
cannot see.

His memories
churned in earth
where roots of love
should be.

His life
is not forgotten
nor the touch – of his
remembered hands.

His respect not lost
for he continues –
to live in me.

What Windows Reveal

Windows show the life
they show the dirt
the sorrow
the shadows – and
they show the whys
the inner moments
all our thoughts
the pains – as
they reflect our eyes
this is what –
windows reveal…..
when we walk by.

What Happens Within

What happens within
happens alone
quandary
delusion
or confusions
of stone.

But a penny found
a perspective seen –
shows new angles to sow.

I Could Have Saved Marilyn

AS with many of my poems, I enjoy writing in a first-person perspective and although I don't often preface my poems, felt this was a good exception to do so. Most men always feel that if they had an opportunity, they could have saved Marilyn Monroe. The vision that came to mind was of a lonely man at his end – similar to Marilyn. He's lying on the bed drinking to his demise, knowing that Marilyn is long dead and the only way to save her is to die. The rest is up to the reader's imagination.

I woke with a plan
...to get drunk;
and drunk again
then when I wake,
dizzy with life....
I would save Marilyn.

Soft and silent
enveloped the pills
of a thousand disguises
but neither us......
had the talent to believe.

When we woke up
life wasn't there

only the cruelty
of what was done
and the secret demon
that seized our differences
and dragged them –
beneath the floor.

Joe sent roses
Arthur wrote plays
while all the other men
believed they to.....
could have saved Marilyn
but it's I who died trying –
at the end.

You Are Worth More

I've lost the light
not seen for days
forgotten words
lost upon the page
with bold letters
standing in the cold
I'm left alone
to shiver – unable
to see my thoughts.

And in the dark I wander
meandering past
these closing walls
a tightness to my breath
feeling for a switch
to change it all.

When truth
reveals the tears
then the light –
reveals it all.

In the corner
stands a friend
watching from a side
when all the mice scurried
they never left the hall.

And with a hug
they said –
this is worth more
than ten-thousand
words.

And you are worth –
more.

The Way of St. James.

I march to you
on feet, bent…..
at humbled knees
and sorrowed
by these cobbled sins.

On a scalloped path
which bears the truth
of many worn souls
that define –
these callused roads.

Once ridden by Napoleon
to find…. what remains
as I to search
to find ones path
on this journey
alone – on The Way
of St. James.

Until The Curtain Falls

Nothing more
springs to mind
as staggered thoughts
stumble…..
across the stage –
where echoes
were once heard
in this now
stagnant hall
and crippled –
are the planks we walk
each groan
a creaking memory
where judgment
now befalls.

Is this the life
we've seen –
when dancing
youthful weans
deprived
or does –
the nourishment
of life survive
until the curtain…..
falls.

Why Can't We

Cover me in your skin
shroud me in your love
surround me
nibble at my thoughts
drink from my heart.

Why can't…..
we watch the rain
just stand alone
forget the day
close our eyes
escape –
and swim away.

Caress my cheeks
kiss my lips
strawberries
sweet wine
at the end of day
why can't we
just pretend
at this social game
of hypocrisy.

Hold me close
forget the crowds
and whisper in my ear.

Why can't we –
just stand here alone
and disappear.

Whisper To Me

Whisper to me
clouds of breath
a tongue full –
of hot melodies.

Warm me
don't take you
away
what about today
and the stars….
of last night.

Take your emotions
infuse them – in me
tell a story
finger tips and windows
open wide.

Don't tell me lies
if I've told you –
everything.

Just whisper…. to me
like a shooting star
make a wish
and I'll be the dream
looking into –
your eyes.

If you just whisper –
to me.

Feelings Without Words

I don't want –
I don't want…..
to open my eyes
to see the night
to see too many questions
when the smoke clears
each one standing there
close at hand
on an empty road
as each day – goes by.

Nothing's changed
but it's not the same
just feelings without
words.

What did I say
what can you say
when you're left in the
dark
no stars to follow
just the light… of pain
to show me the way.

I don't want…..
to open my eyes
because nothing's
changed
but it's not the same
it's all just feelings –
without words.

Teardrops Of Rain

Call me –
tell me what to say
under street lamps of stars
walking in your teardrops
of rain.

Car lights and memories
blurs which flash on by
deep thoughts of
yesterday
call me – and tell me why.

Until then I'll walk alone
and walk until I've gone
too far
and then I'll turn around
perhaps I'll see you there
standing in a phone booth
– calling me.

Car lights and memories
blurs which flash on by
deep thoughts of
yesterday
call me – and tell me why.

I'll tell you that my feet
are wet

my soul has washed away
sidewalks and gutters
and grey newspapers – of
yesterday
Call me – tell me what to
say.

While I sit here and wring
my hands
on these old storied palms
lines and broken tea-bags
a worn life, which leaves a
tale
can I call you – and tell
you why.

As car lights and
memories
blurs which flash on by
deep thoughts of
yesterday
I better call – before I've
walked too far.

Standing under street
lamps of stars
walking…..
in your teardrops of rain.

I've Forgotten Nothing

What thoughts are forgotten
what narratives have disappeared
how far are we from yesterday
if today has gone unheard.

So talk about your solitude
dissecting life and fears
such a wonderful disguise it is
which you've developed over years.

But if I could reach beyond the stars
to touch your gentle cheek
to dodge the slaughter of your tongue
and feel your hips beneath.

Then all those lost forgotten hopes
vacations of a dislocated heart
compromises and despairs
would be ours to keep

So I've forgotten nothing then
and remember yesterday
and what I've forgotten doesn't matter
nor does the narrative.

Dry The Tears of Others

What potential do you see
in the midnight dreams of solitude
where you paint time on canvas eyes
to only watch the moments dry
on your grey beached inlets…. of eternity.

Why count time with shadowed hands
when you can watch the earth sink –
then watch…… the sun-rise.

Close your eyes, witness freedom
sail the earth and disregard the ticking sand
forsake the swatches – painted by the man
so you can feel the hands of others.

Now what potential do you see
in the midnight dreams of solitude
where you paint time on canvas eyes
to dry the tears of others.

This Tangled Life

What is this tangled life you
feel, when the clapper
strikes the bell - can you not
feel me inside your pain
or am the ghost that
wrinkles life, a cockle
beneath your shell.

Then you should have
looked a little longer
and felt the baying moon
you should have watched
the mirror and seen the
shadows dance, as each
creak felt the groan.

Tell me -
did you feel the stretch of
burning walls and the touch
of caressing tongues
did you feel the heat of
passion, or the burning of
your lungs.

Did you wake with me at
half past three
to see the window, lonely
by the sill - watching lifeless
minds walk-by
as I deconstructed your
complexities and kissed you
then – free of will.

Dance with me
forget the dirty window
or the smudges on the wall
footprints on the ceiling
we knew the room beneath
the bed - was going to be
too small.

Tangle me in this tangled
life, until you comprehend
my will
then splash me with your
eyelids and I'll pour you
into me and drink you until
I'm full.

When We Meet Again

Upon the rays of morning's sun
are the cheers, of all the loves we've won
and the brightness deep of mind is set
so when the turn of life has come
we'll not wither as the dust befalls
but remember well, as our eyes close in rest.

For I've dreamt the dream a thousand times
and felt the freshness of your pale loves skin
on tenderness of lips, from heart to breath
which I now recall with clarity,
as I view these translucent hands.

But on the morn, not so long ago
when your passion, once set the time of day
would bring rise to my mornings sun
and your smile would set the stage
for those rose coloured cheeks
would blossom as we frolicked in our play.

So now, I watch the evening set
and count each remembered star
for there are no tears to weep
as I rest my weary head
and leave these roots behind,
as our life will surely bloom
on that day - when we meet again.

Tomorrow - May Be My Last

Windswept fields of dancing wheat
breezes with a hint of salt and sea
but I also see the shadows, which
loom upon the mountain peaks
and the avalanches, which gather beneath.

For man is but a stone, when pushed
and clamorous is this wretched heap
for blood is what he gives to live
and death is but another man's demise.

As today, I've seen the sun
and I've laid upon the grass
tonight I'll drink the stars of hope
for tomorrow - may be my last.

In The Mirror

Have you ever seen the man
unfocused...
clearly a recluse unto himself
watching another -
in the mirror.

Closing doors, behind remorse
cursing at himself
without any recognition
of this person -
in the mirror.

Now shattered are his thoughts
without the clarity of hope
as the eyes recognise the rejection
of the others reflection -
in the mirror.

As his conscious walks by
and screams
what happened to his
pride
what's there to hide
then let's go find it -
in the mirror.

Because everything he
needs to see
is right there in the open
watching him,
 from inside out
deep inside -
the mirror.

The Only One

She is the one
with glint of rays,
which inspires
upon a solitary look
of her sparkled eyes -
many men's desires.

She is the one
that fortifies the stars
so they can....
embrace the night
with her serenity -
and smile.

She is the one
of eloquence and grace,
which brings tranquility
upon my heart.

She is the one
that bears witness
to the softness of my soul
as her charms,
places a sheath
upon my sword.

For she is -
the only one.

You're Unaware

You stole my tongue
crossed the borderland
tied my hands
bound me to you
and set my words
into a run
what is the truth
of your lies
if you've broken my spirit
all for what -
just your fun
as you sat and stared
because you missed the point
and you're unaware.

It's My Soul

If I call a thousand times
and all I see are shadows
with only sounds of ricochets
and echoes.... to be heard -
what more should be said
if all you do is hide-away
then there's nothing left to say.

But when you hear the voices
in the darkness of the night
those shadows.....
are no longer yours - but mine
as it's my soul
which now reflects the light.

* * * * * *

She heard me age
by reading all my groans
written on those tattered pages
born from every day -
within a life.....
stripped of chapters
each word written -
for her.

* * * * * *

Reminded Me - Of Life

There....
by the mainstream of life
is the willow tree,
overhanging branches,
streetlamps
and cascading beams
of light.

As floods of souls walked by
the air filled with words
on occasion -
despair is heard.

Then all sound stops!

For a solitary tear -
smashed into the
pavement
but no one hears
except the tender leaves
of the willow.....
frolicking in the wind.

Reach for me -
feel the silk

touch my cheek
let them all walk by
as I stand frozen
in that moment, which
stood alone in time
a willow leaf -
touched me.

And reminded me -
of life.

The Promised Land

You know where your heart lays
it's beneath me
wrapped in my arms;
we are bound to each other
as is the water to the ship.

So open your sails
feel the flood of mercy's
warm breath -
envelop my tongue
till your lungs expand
and then expel your joy
letting your feet dance
as your skin
electrifies the air.

Then grasp the sheets
bear down on the wind -
float upon the waves
as if you were one...
and I the other -
as we sail hard towards
the Promised Land.

Steal My Night

Where do we go
when all the roads are bare -
how do you feel
when we've crisscrossed -
everywhere.

Have you seen this path
is it ours
or everyone's before.

Now what
where do we go from here.

If you close your eyes
will another day break
will another road
appear.

Or will long shadows
cast there sky on you
or will they break the path -
of me.

And steal my night....away.

I Love You Anyway

Her desires
are but a breath away
as is my home
with its quickened pulse
a lovers deep emotions -
where it all began.

But she always leaves me
tangled with my thoughts.....
I'm left alone
with my lover
on my mind.

She never opens up
a quick mistaken peek
then she closes all her doors.

Is our love so hard, to
define
I only try to make her
smile
she's always on my mind
even when she's standing
right behind..... her door.

Why won't you open up
you're but a breath away
just you and your other
lover
yet I love you anyway.

I love you.... anyway.

Just Yesterday

Into my dreams, I wandered
to see an old friend -
and there she was...
as if it were... just yesterday.

And sometimes in the morning
like two days just before
when everything was easy
I only had to blink
then I'd be day-dreaming...
as if it were... just yesterday.

Such simple thoughts
of what could have been
and the love of holding hands
in a world of make-believe
where if I reached out
she'd be there...
as if it were... just yesterday.

So sweet dreams are these
when she once thought of me
in her day-dreaming days
before all these years
have gone by -
but when I close my eyes
she's always there...
as if it were... just yesterday.

Feel His Beat of Air

His heart is right
just misplaced - unfound
but when it pounds,
it's too loud for her to hear.

So with his hands
he writes a pantomime
but her eyes are closed
and unfocused are his thoughts
as tears run down his cheeks.

Franticly he waves at her
anxious with despair....
he draws these pictures
so she can listen with her heart
and feel his beat of air.

Everlasting Sleep

With a single glimpse
she imprisons' me
tangled in her web
a crinkled gleam
I'm caught off guard
but pleasantly surprised
by the warmth of poison
dripping off her smile.

She envelops me
wrapped within
the multitude of charms
and sins
disarming fears
as a single tear escapes
to the peace of love
and everlasting..... sleep.

My Harmony

She is sunlight
a ray of hope
within my veins
which my heart....
drinks in.

Her eyes
a symphony -
an instrumental
composition
each movement
composed for me.

I can feel her hands
silk on ivory skin
each touch
a key
a single note -
she is my song
my sunlight.

My harmony.

Invisible To You

Why am I invisible to you
you're always just a stranger
when I'm on the inside of me
looking outside for you.

Then time goes by
even when your arms are wide
the numbers don't add up
it's all about convenience
just an infinity
but in the end, the answer's just a lie.

Now all the words are difficult
the many questions end in why
but some words never change
you're just a person
some days you pretend to care
and other days you hide.

Why am I invisible to you
when I'm on the inside of me
that's when I'm looking outside for you.
You know the way the world turns
you've spun their before
when you're upside down

I've always tried to hold up the sky
and blow away the clouds.

So why am I invisible
when it really should be you.

I've Chosen My Fears

I've chosen my fears
whether I've lost - or won
walked in circles
or held back the tears.

But on cold sunny days
when confused by....
the feeling of rain
I'll still love you -
in the end.

So take my hand
understand
how I got here
and the consequences
the ridiculous
and the stares.

Weird blue skies
which swim in the air
to release the night
as dreams come on
and remain the same
in the hope -
that you'll still hold me.

Whether I've lost - or won
I've chosen my fears.

Let Them Sleep

Let them sleep
beneath the shivers of the trees
as the guns bellow their salute
to the fallen mourning leaves
and November cries colours to the lost
a tartan blanket for the brave
so we who remain
shall warm our souls
wrapped in memories
of brothers, sisters, fathers, mothers -
and friends.

Let them sleep
so we who remain
can now guard them.

NOTE: This poem was a last minute entry for the book, which I wrote for Remembrance Day, November 11th 2012.

Standing By My Side

I never heard your words
they changed each time I turned
but when I spun around
no longer were you there.

Then with nothing much to do
I sat and watched the stars
until I saw the moon
in hope, I'd dream of you.

What have you done
what did you say
I tried to change
but never heard your words
each phrase became too much
you never sat around
and each day became too long.

So I stood and walked away
towards the ocean and the spray
it was then I heard your words
with the clarity of mind
and when I spun around
there you were -
standing by my side.

Returned To Calm

She never ran
but was pushed by the wind
this blow to her heart
a lost ship on high seas
turmoil tossed in sins
a telescopic gaze
looking for the calm
as the battered sheets
tied to the worn rigging of life
now feel torn….. within.

Can you taste the salt
now dried upon my skin
for there are no more tears
and nothing left to shed
as life's seas -
have now returned to calm.

A Penny For Your Thoughts

How many pennies do you need
will they feed your wants
or starve your desires
find you friends
or buy you love.

Will your skin turn copper
will your veins turn to gold
or a weight to drag you down
as your face turns old -
how many pennies do you need.

If you're lost - can you leave a trail
to find your way back home
write a list - so you can watch it grow
where else can you go from here
when your pennies disappear
and you've lost your way.

Can you believe this curse
when you wake up
in the middle of your day
you have no friends
they've all been paid
can anything be worse.

What changes can you make
can you spell or count it out
I'd really like to know
and I'll pay
so here's a penny…..
for your thoughts.

Behind Me

You're just a step behind
as I watch you crawl along
this shadow
an outer layer of sin -
which haunts me.

So who is the victim
is it you or I
and what tales,
have you dragged along.

Can you feel the sun
as you continue….
to taunt me
a secret which burns
between you… and I.

So how can I -
wash away the doubt
when you're one step closer
behind me.

A Series of Moments (Micro-poems)

With each whispered sin – my heart……. skipped….. a beat

Wisps of clouds – remind me…. of her – as soft subtleties…. of memories – float by

You seduce each word…. as it slips past your lips – then each word….
seduces me

Can I stroke you – like I stroke… each note – and… if I play you – will you sing… for me

The cadence… of your voice… lulls me – till I realize... that I'm holding… my breath – can I kiss you – and touch my soul…to your lips

If I am your ship….. then all I desire - is to be married…. to the sea

I gave you what I had – until my tears…. turned to blood – and then….. I gave you more

I am a tree that leans; my roots are bare – I can feel the rain - but hope for the splash… of the heated sun – while I wait for your…return

She stands sentinel - a guardian of my heart – protecting….. what is hers

He extends an olive branch.... but she pretends - that she was born.... without hands

The sun rises to see the dawn of day – but will his heart rise – to breathe in the dawn.... of life

I raced through the shadows – until I seen.... her smile

She was.... deliciously poised – suspended in his eyes – he licked his lips – to a delicacy.... he graved

Write me a note of love.... and place it in the clock - then we'll wait and see - if it stands.... the test of time

I'm in paradise – when you touch my mind – and when your eyes.... touch my face

All I want to do.... is run to her – and chase the sadness – from her eyes

She takes me.... into her heart – deeper....... then I thought.... I'd ever go

I can hear her thoughts - and she rapes my mind..... daily

When I'm with you – you are my heaven – my solitude – my mountain top - you take me to a place – where I love you

He sits.... lost between the clouds – his vision is unclear – to only see her eyes – would be to see the brightness – of the sun

If you looked, if you only looked, you would see the gentle eyes, the torrid rains and the mixture of the love and pains... of me

My soul aches, with visions in the night; dragging past my sleepless eyes.... haunting images, which cry - for sight

When you went away – I watched you go.... and I lost the time of day – then I lost myself.... in this calendar.... of memories

He lost himself – his balance off, he went askew – and she watched.... as he tumbled..... away

Two butterflies – surrounded by the stars – that's what you are to me – the fragile grace of beauty – and the sparkle... of your moonlit eyes

The morning rains flail – and the ground jumps in surprise – as the dark clouds laugh

She hides like a thief.... who stole my heart – but sad..... is that she runs away – from hers

In the silence of my day.... she was never seen – but her sweet whispers.... always heard

The scent of her....told the story – before her parted lips..... ever spoke.... a word

He was translucent... to her – as she watched.... every thought.... appeared

He guards his tongue – behind this jailed smile – which belays…. his imprisoned words

Everyday…. I'd wait – looking out to sea – and hope for remnants of memories…. of her – to wash ashore… to me

I stood…. watching – and so did time – and everyone and thing…. was still – when she walked….. by

Wash me~~~~ in your sea of thoughts – and drink me – like the earth drinks in the sun

Her life is a theatre – a play of will – but what role… have I played – or am I just a prop, now lost….. upon this stage

Her tongue….. caresses me – with these sweet words of bliss – then next…. she cuts me deep – like a double-edged---- sword

A glass home upon the hill – where no stones can roll – but when looked up upon – you can see… where they've been thrown

I am moored to her – she is the ocean….. and I the shore – she laps at me, with her sweet gentle lips – and I fall….. into her

Each mornings dawn…. I wake to find - the enlightenment….of you – you are the beauty… of each waking day

She consumed me, with each touch…. of her skin – a licking flame, which devours me – I'm just the fuel that feeds… her passions heat

A gravity … which pulls me – I am bound to her…… like I am tied to the earth – and nowhere else… do I wish to be

To kiss a women, is to kiss the passion of the morning sun – to feel the warmth of her desire – as two souls – melt…… into one

To kiss a women, is to kiss the passion of the morning sun – to feel the warmth of her desire – as two souls – melt…… into one

Pain is but a suffering word – which binds itself to thee – untie such wordless ropes and bind your bodies aches – to me

I shall cover you with silk skin… to smooth away the roughness of the day – and kiss your eyes – to wash away your tears

If I were the wind – then I shall whisper to your hair – and tease you with a gentle breeze – so that you know – that I am near

Put your hand…. on me – feel my chest – as you ignite the fire…. which now, warms you – in the heat…. of your desire

Take these old heart strings….. and tune them – then gently pluck away…. until you hear them play…. your song

Use your hands…. and paint me – then hold…. my hands – as I paint… forget-me-nots – on you

Raw emotions – these torn strips….. which bare me – exposing….. a depth – beneath this shell…. of skin

The parchment drowns…. like her – it can…. no longer breathe – life pours….. sins… which stain the page – and him

You stepped out of line – and tore the wire – that connected us – now how frayed…. are we

Her words were dry – as they fell upon his tongue – like burnt ashes – they choked him

Dark circles – is a portrait of her – which he draws…. beneath his eyes

You are my alter – you are my penance – You are…. my sacred sins

Into the valley rode the mind, in search…. of the black dogs - which taunted him – but it was their howling – that led him to the abyss

Tie your hands~~~~ in knots around me – bind yourself…. to my naked flesh – and I will be forever moored….. to you

You preach, but I see no pulpit – but your staccato of words – are no different than a gun – as they leave damage – everywhere

Bare me your inner soul – purge yourself….on me – for it's you that carries this weight – but if you ask… I shall carry you

What is sleep without rest – this torment…. that bears a deeper pain; if you peel away the darkness – perhaps the light…will remain

Into the sea, he cast the stones, to watch the rocks… just drown – for they cannot skip – when the waves just overwhelm ~~~

The ink was spilt – splattered on the page – now all the words are mixed – a pool of thoughts – now… in disarray

By the midnight candle….. he watches the drips – as life just runs….. away – by the dawn of morning – only a puddle sits

Don't feel the flesh – but touch the bones – its ten-past midnight – and I'm looking for you – to find…. my soul… your home

I've searched for you…. forever – in the field of dreams – but now my visions cloudy – or is this just…. the reality

On this board…. I am a pawn - who feels the weight of queens - no longer do I fit this realm - which has seen the days… of kings

I walk the streets – to see the world – but I am just an actor….upon this stage – and when I close my eyes – the audience… disappears

I wore her……like silk fabric – each subtle movement…. was luxurious – and then….. we kissed

You are…. the air – my ground – you are the sun – you are my breath – my foundation – you are my light – you are…. my love

You are my river.... and I the smooth rocks... on the bed – you are my sea... and I the sand – I am your words... and you are my truth

You are.... my paper – your skin..... bound to me – my spine erect.... holds you... – my arms.... cover.... protect... and fold over... you

Crumpled paper – my heart on a page – what does she throw...... away – but these little pieces...... of me

With a stone in each hand – I weigh us – one me – the other..... for the window – a reflection of my heart – and who I used to be

Lie with me – talk to me – – – kiss me – – – temp me – to fall in love.... with you

She is my flower – and I am.... the spring – my heart is the sun – and her smile.... is loves bloom

His mood swings.... like a pendulum – once side the light – the other.................. the end

What curse is fate – when hammered on the door – if it is not love..... that calls – then call me...... no more

I wear her... like a warm scarf – sleek and wrapped around – but it's the pattern of her..... I enjoy – as she is woven.... into me

Listen – as these fingers – strum..... different strings – and the eyes watch.... and fret – can you hear... the hidden notes

One frolics – a follies by design – but sadly…… the other….
only sees the clown

He wears his emotions like a hat – or a coat of translucent skin – she sees his heart – but does she see…. the reality of truth….. within

Your skin has no gender - your colour…. defines no race - the language of our bodies - bear the weight…. of our minds grace

I am the cover of a book – hard….. and inviting – but all the mystery…. lust and desires - is what lays writing….. between

I swirl my tongue – to entertain – the flesh… of her words – but deconstructed outbursts… of moans – is all that I can hear

FOR YOU

The night I looked at you - I found the reality………. of my dreams

I show her my weaknesses…. and she cares enough - to understand my strengths

She knows me, my life, my pain, my inner thoughts - why I do, what I do - she gets to see… the private - in me

When I found her - I found a "peace" of heaven

She grounds me - she is my earth

The structure of her mind, supports me - she is… my home

Her one hand steadies my soul - the other - my heart

My favourite time of day - is with you

All day I've wondered…… where does she fit… into my life; then I realised…… I was holding my breath - she is my breath, my lungs, my heart………. my life

I move around you… like you're my sun – but in truth…… you've become – my world

All I want to do… is to sit on stones steps…… and drink in life… as it saunters by – that would be a perfect day… with you

She is – the road I wish to travel – and the journey….. I never wish to end

A Short Story

Who am I?

I am a soldier!

Two weeks after I turned 17, I was in basic training, then off to join my beloved regiment, The Royal Canadian Regiment (The RCR) as an infantier. I served for 25-years in three different vocations within the forces.

In 1988 I was on-board a destroyer escort, which was tied up in the San Francisco Bay Wharf area. With a night off, I ventured out to explore the city. While heading back to the ship that evening, I heard the most amazing music and followed the notes; now nestled on my bar stool I enjoyed my favourite pastime – people-watching.

I love watching people and how animated some are, while others are so reserved and the whole host of those in-between. I recall two-lawyers arguing away, some guy talking about his teaching position to this woman, politics from another and the guy beside me not saying a word. In total there were about 15 of us stationed around the bar, sipping life. I was happy!

However, being a Gemini, I tend to become bored at times, and although sitting still, my mind was whirling at a rapid pace.

"Time for a poem!"

Note: *when I was writing on Twitter, whether titled as "RefugeInsomniac" or as "Daves_Ink", many would note that when I posted a new poem, I always started with "A Poem" followed by the poems title. That simple phrase was born that night in that small San Francisco pub.*

At the top of a new napkin, I wrote "A POEM", and then I wrote the first line and passed it with the pen, to the gentleman beside me. I was ready; I had my little speech about a social experiment prepared, but he never said a single word, not even a sigh. I was 6-foot 2 inches tall and weighed about 195-pounds. This man to my left had at least 2-inches on me and a good 60 pounds, if not more; he simply wrote a line and passed it along. I couldn't stop smiling – a poem was being written from an eclectic group of people as I've ever seen.

Some would pause, some would shrug and point to me, and others just scribbled a line and passed it along as though it was a normal thing to do. Everyone wrote something, this in itself amazed me. I finished my beer, collected "our "poem and left. I never read the poem that night, I wanted to savour it.

Two life lessons were learnt from this experience and one poignantly enforced as we sailed towards open sea the next morning. The ocean is unforgiving and it relished in

reminding me of that fact, as it squeezed every ounce of sour beer from my belly – death was looking like a pretty damn good alternative; a sailor, I most certainly am not.
More importantly, while enjoying my supper of dry crackers and gravol, in the comfort of my bunk, I noticed the napkin and recalled the poem.

To be honest I was unsure of what I'd find, or what I even expected to find. But I know for sure that it was nothing like I had imagined.

I suppose I had this vision of magical words which danced from line to line; a great ballroom, filled to the brim, each person from a different culture, each line forced to blend as their hands met and their thoughts twirled at the end of the pen. It had to be that way; each person was different, from education to life's story, right up until that very moment we were all gathered around that wooden bar in San Francisco.

What I read was a very simple poem, with simple words, yet it had a great depth of meaning. In the army I was always taught to write reports with brevity and clarity in mind, the latter taking precedent. That's what the poem was – it was a story in its simplest form and it made sense to me.

My style of poetry changed that night and I tossed complexity out of my bunk and off the ship.

My poems are simple – and that's it really; some work, some don't, some I think are good, while others in my opinion fail to convey the emotions I was feeling when I wrote them. As with each line written that night in a small pub near the wharf, each meant something different to the person who wrote them. But that's another lesson in itself – it's not the emotions I felt while writing my words that counted, it's the emotions that each reader feels when they read them.

I hope that you can find at least one poem to enjoy.

Cheers,
David

My Great-Great-Great Grandfather

As a general note of interest, my Great-Great-Great Grandfather, was the Gailic poet, The Bard John MacLean. Born, 8 January 1787, in Caolas, Tiree Scotland, and died 26 January 1848 in Addington Forks, Antigonish County, Nova Scotia Canada. Although I can certainly not be compared to his poetic greatness, I would venture to say that I may owe my meagre rambling attempt to scratch pen to parchment in some distant manner to him.

For more information, please visit the Government of Nova Scotia Canada Virtual Archives site on John MacLean: http://www.gov.ns.ca/nsarm/virtual/gaelic/archives.asp?ID=31

The following is the first verse of his famous poem, A' Choille Ghruamach, or The Gloomy Forest.

A' Choille Ghruamach
Gu bheil mi' m'onrachd 'sa choille ghruamaich,
Mo smaointinn luaineach, cha tog mi fonn:
Fhuair mi' n t-àite so' n aghaidh nàduir,
Gu' n d'thréig gach tàlanta bha 'nam cheann:
Cha dean mi òran a' chur air doigh ann,
Nuair ni mi toiseachadh bidh mi trom:
Chaill mi Ghàidhlig seach mar a b' àbhaist dhomh,
Nuair a bha mi 'san dùthaich thall.

English version:

Gloomy Forest
Lone, brooding mid the gloom of forest verdure,
My moods are fitful, and my soul is wan:
I've got this place which stands at strife with nature,
And all my native powers of mind are gone.
I cannot now construct a song with order,
And if I should begin the heart grows sore:
The Gaelic too, I've lost, as used o'er yonder,
In that far mountain land in years of yore.

* * * * * *

Authors Notes

Please note, that I will not provide a brief understanding behind all poems, but just s few.

Poems:

AN1) **When The Wolves Howl**: When I first joined Twitter my name was "RefugeInsomniac". This moniker was based on the fact that (1) I do not sleep well – in fact on average, manage only 1 to 4-hours of interspersed sleep per-night and (2) based on a quote from Leonard Cohen "The last refuge of the insomniac is a sense of superiority to the sleeping world.". So while trying to figure out what to enter for my Twitter Bio, I doodled out this little poem :-)

AN2) **Shadows**: A soldiers dream.

AN3) **Do I Still Exist**: This poem was written for a young man who had just hung himself in the barracks.

A soldier's life is not always what a young knight thinks it will be; when the dawn has passed and the shadows come out to play, a different fairytale is written – and each ending, is never the same.

AN4) **Days Ago:** In 1979 I returned from the Middle East, and within months, was posted to Canadian Forces Base Baden-Soellingen, Rheinmünster, West Germany. This poem is a reflection of those days as I was trying to adjust.

AN5) **Metal Closet**: The first sign of Post Traumatic Stress Disorder rear's it's head.

AN6) **Tattoo's**: When I first presented this poem, a few individuals found it somewhat confusing. However, I am not very partial to outlining poems, as each person develops their own connection, based off their own feelings at the moment or how they relate to the words.

Regardless, I'll break this down a bit: the military reference to the term tattoo dates back to the 17th century where the garrison would send Drummers into the towns at 21:30 hrs (9:30PM) each evening to inform the soldiers that it was time to return to barracks. The process was known as doe den tap toe (Dutch for "turn off the tap"), an instruction to innkeepers to stop serving beer and send the soldiers home for the night.

Then we have a clear reference to the term of tattoos, which many willing apply to their skin with indelible ink and then those unfortunate others who had numbered tattoos driven into their very souls.

The rest is up to the reader.

AN7) **Swish Swish... swish**: A piece of paper stuck on the bottom of my shoe, while out walking the dogs :-)

AN8) **No Longer Does He Care**: I wrote this poem for an old army buddy who suffers from Post Traumatic Stress Disorder (PTSD) and associated alcoholism. He had recently been evicted from his apartment, was refusing help and subsequently living on the streets.

My family and I made a collective decision to bring this man into our home. Although, it was morally the right thing to do for a friend, I can assure you it was a difficult challenge and one I would never recommend. Suitable accommodations and help were found, but his struggles continue.

Please, if you ever see a soldier struggling, don't judge him/her; they only did what our governments have asked of them, they did it well and we should be proud of them. Any issues you have should be directed towards the government, not the soldier.

Unfortunately, the soldier's real battles begin when they return home – so try to understand.

This poem was written on a very hot summer afternoon, just after I found my friend drunk on Listerine in a park - we talked for an hour or so, then he stumbled off and said…. "No Longer Does He Care".

AN9) **Magical Mind Of Mine**: While growing up in the sixties little was known, specifically within the educational sectors about nurturing kids with learning difficulties, whom I was one of. Let's just say, that I spent many days standing in a corner of the classroom and many more days wandering the Niagara escarpment with a book or drawing pad in one hand and a mitt full of dreams in the other. Regardless, here we are many years later and over the last few years and several unofficial tests later, it's fairly clear that I fit nicely into the lower spectrum of the Aspergers Syndrome scale. And to be honest, it's finally nice to know, and more importantly to understand and have explanations for so many things from over the years.

AN10) **A Broken Heart**: Remembering my first true love – and subsequent broken heart.

AN11) **I Wince**: My wife suffers from Multiple Sclerosis and there is nothing I can do. Quite often the pain in her legs in unbearable.

AN12) **Raining Room**: My wife also suffers from intense Migraines, especially during her menstrual cycle – such pain, coupled with the pain of her MS often leaves her in tears. She'll certainly hate that I've mentioned any of this, but I feel speaking openly about such problems, which I'm sure many others deal with, is important.

AN13) **Two-Cents Then**: This poem has many references, which I'll allow the reader to sort out for themselves, but it primarily focuses on, not just politicians or nations, but the need for people as a whole to speak out and address tragedies against humanity.

AN14) **Flat and Simple**: A young boys dream and a soldier reality.

The interpretation of all other poems is now left up to you :-)

* * * * * *

Thank you for taking the opportunity in supporting my poetry, it means a great deal to me and I am forever thankful.

And now that we've reached the end of this journey, perhaps we can share a refreshing glass of wine together....

Thank you again; Cheers, David

Index of Titles

Acknowledgments 1
Introduction 1

POEMS 1
My Saturated Stems 2
Loves Due 4
When The Wolves Howl 5
Shadows 6
Taste The Fear 8
Do I Still Exist 9
Days Ago 10
Metal Closet 11
Forever Longed 12
Silver Moon 13
All These Dots 14
Unlike The Seed 15
Just Listen 16
Eyes Open 17
Words 18
Sand 19
Swallows Even Me 21
Still Just Me 22
Breathless 23
To Me 24
Languish 25
Close my eyes 26
Tattoo's 28
I Remember Them 29
Concentration 30
An Old Stone Well 31
We'll Be Fine 32
Lonely Thoughts 33

Just Her And I, And Me 34
Swish Swish… swish 35
Just Another Gnome 36
Keeping Me From Rest . 37
Leap of Faith 39
No Matter What I Say ...40
Twelve beers 41
Twenty-one 43
One Breath at a Time 44
Shattered 46
I Remember You 48
In The Leaves 50
My Life 51
Words we spoke 52
In The Waiting Room 53
A Wall 54
Spilt Emotions 55
Let The Roses Grow 56
Lives Apart 57
I'll Just Stand Still ..58
Summer's Rain 60
Mind-fields 61
Close my Eyes and
Breathe 62
Pale Edges 63
"No Longer Does He
Care" 65
She Drank Time 66
Sweet Reverie 67
The Darkness Doesn't
Know 68
On Top of Tall 69

249

Violin Strings 70	On This Side Of My Head
Residual Goodbyes 73	 113
I Hear A Bird That	Call the Clan - For Me 114
Whispers 74	Written For Tomorrow
Mornings Dawn 76	 115
May Bloom 77	Deep Within 116
The Light Shines 79	A Mirrored Look 117
Snarled 80	The Soul Of A Child ... 118
She Drew A Circle 82	Two-Cents Then 119
Magical Mind of Mine .. 85	Ever Wonder 120
His Mind 86	Afternoon Sail 121
On the Brink 87	To Read and Deduce... 123
The Scattered Mind 89	Flat And Simple 125
Feathers Float Away 90	A Bell Rung 126
Unexpected Moments ... 91	A Heavy Chest 128
Change Must Come 92	Unwrapped is the Scarf
Steel Cogs 94	 129
For Me 95	Two Hands Make The
Draw Me 96	Time 130
A Broken Heart 97	How Many Doors 131
Nights Are Best To Crush	You And Me 132
Their Hearts 99	They Grind Me 133
Passion 101	Sour Love 134
Just A Heartbeat Away	If I Reached Out 135
.... 102	You Are That Woman. 136
I Drank You In 103	Love Would Be Free.... 137
Drifting Away 104	Into My Tree 139
She Pulls Me 105	Ink Stains and You 140
I Wince 106	Who Will Pick the Apples
Raining Room 108	Now 141
Shoes That Walk 109	Can I 142
What He Had Lost 112	Just Beneath The Sun .. 143

He withers in the storm 144	What Tomorrow Brings 168
What if the sky turned grey 144	Hidden 169
A Connection 144	The Blank Page 170
Carry me across the ocean 145	Exposed 171
He wakes up in a fog .. 145	Beating Drum 172
Don't come back to me 145	You Can Paint Me 173
When time has lost the 146	I Understand 174
It's easy to lose people 146	Feed The Fragments of Your Soul 175
Every Whisper Is Heard 147	She Pushed Me 176
An Invisible Ghost 148	Nurtures Life 176
When I've Lost You 149	Stars 177
I Was Left To Listen 151	In The Mist 178
Back Home 152	Whispers Love 179
What is Friendship 153	I Hear 180
Time of Day 155	Atop The Pier 181
How Dangerous 155	Those Hues - of Blue ... 182
A Constellated Mesh ... 156	The Show 183
Once More 157	Why Is The Water Still 184
I Want To Tumble 158	Divisions 185
Away 160	What I'm Not 186
Lake of Tears 161	Only The Silence Remains 187
To See The Bridges 163	A Dot Upon A Page 188
Deeper Than The Flesh 164	Un-Engaging Is The Sky 189
His Last Breath 165	Abacus Mind 190
Freedom of the Sands . 166	Jukebox Eyes 191
In All The Faith 167	Even On The Darkest Nights 192
	A Set Of Stairs 193

When The Pendulum Falls 194
Drenched 195
Yesterday....................... 195
His Memories................ 196
What Windows Reveal 197
What Happens Within 197
I Could Have Saved Marilyn 198
You Are Worth More .. 199
The Way of St. James. . 200
Until The Curtain Falls 201
Why Can't We............... 202
Whisper To Me 203
Feelings Without Words 204
Teardrops Of Rain........ 205
I've Forgotten Nothing 206
Dry The Tears of Others 207
This Tangled Life.......... 208
When We Meet Again 209
Tomorrow - May Be My Last 210

In The Mirror 211
The Only One................ 212
It's My Soul 213
The Promised Land..... 215
Steal My Night.............. 216
I Love You Anyway 217
Just Yesterday 218
Feel His Beat of Air 219
Everlasting Sleep.......... 220
My Harmony 220
Invisible To You 221
I've Chosen My Fears . 222
Let Them Sleep 223
Standing By My Side .. 224
Returned To Calm........ 225
A Penny For Your Thoughts....................... 226
Behind Me 227

A Series of Moments (Micro-poems) 228
FOR YOU 237
A Short Story 238
My Great-Great-Great Grandfather...................... 242
Authors Notes 244

www.ingramcontent.com/pod-product-compliance
Lightning Source LLC
Chambersburg PA
CBHW051750040426
42446CB00007B/299